MISANDRY EXPOSED!

An Exposé of The Sexism &

Double Standards Against Men

In Our Gynocentric Culture

Table Of Contents

1 - Introduction To Misandry And Gynocentrism

I was raised by a first wave feminist and taught about equality and women's rights growing up. That was decades ago though, back when men and women could get along. Over the last decade I have watched feminism come to dominate the political and social worlds, even the world of social media, the dating world, the sex ed world, and other niche communities, such as the online dating industry, the porn industry, and the Kink/BDSM world, and basically any social community or industry where male/female sexual dynamics are the focus. This has made the social world at large a gynocentric culture which caters to women at the expense of men.

Since the third and fourth waves of feminism have emerged (which are more about women winning the battle of the sexes than equality,) there has been a growing trend of women who feel a need to emasculate men and make men feel like less of a man. This is most commonly and done with the phrase we are all too familiar with of "you are not a real man". We have all heard this phrase used to such an extent that it has become cliché. There is no good reason for it, and they only do this in order to coerce a man to try to behave the way they want, by attaching his sense of identity as a man to the behavior they want him to exhibit, and a break down of said identity to his non-conformity. This is similar to gas lighting and is an incredibly toxic sociopathic thing to do to someone. But women these days seem to love emasculating men because it not only is a great form of ammunition they can use to try to get the man to conform to their wishes, but it makes them feel powerful. This a very dark trait that is ironic because it is most often done by women who have a feminist "girl power" attitude, but yet they are completely ignoring the fact that this is actually an extremely and extraordinarily sexist thing to say to someone. This is so far beyond any form of sexism that feminism has rebelled against.

The misogyny of the past has never attempted to break down women's sense of identity in their gender and make them feel like less of a woman. While the phrase "not a real man" is so common it is cliché, there is no such phrase for women, you simply will not be able to produce a memory of a man saying "you are not a real woman". Because men do not use emotional manipulation and abuse or try to break down women's sense of being female just because of her non-compliance. When a man want's a woman to comply with him he will use rational discourse and debate to attempt to bring her to realize why doing things his way is beneficial so that she can decide to do so consciously of her own free will.

Trying to break down someone's sense of identity simply to manipulate them and get them to comply with you is extremely destructive to their mental health and wellbeing, and is incredibly unethical and immoral because of it. It is a narcissistic, sociopathic, and fascist, in fact it is the type of thing that the Nazi's did to the Jews during the holocaust, in which they tried to remove their humanity and reduce them down to domesticated farm animals. But yet women do this to men and get away with it. Women treat men like domesticated pets. Women who want a man to comply will try to take away not only his free will but his identity and sense of self esteem and manliness. Unfortunately for men this causes serious mental health issues in a man and can make him depressed and even suicidal. The suicide rates among men have always been higher than among women, and now men are begin oppressed by women worse than women ever were by men, and women feel justified in doing it, because they have infiltrated politics and created a gynocentric socio-political system that panders to women's every whim, even when they are misandristic, or even fascist.

Yet the high suicide rates of men has never been seen as a problem to women. Women like the idea of men sacrificing themselves for women and children, that is seen as the main thing men can contribute to the greater good, is their lives, and if not that, then their livelihood while they are living. Suicide rates were only seen as an issue recently when the far lower suicide rates of women started to raise a little. Just as how when men are putting themselves at risk in military, police, fire, etc. and routinely getting injured, losing their health, or getting killed it is seen as normal, but when women start doing so it becomes a big deal that women are risking everything and they start needing special treatment to protect them. Just as how there is so much awareness and community support created for the problem of breast cancer that women have, but yet testicular and prostate cancer which kills far more men than breast cancer does women never gets any type of awareness or community support, because women don't care that men are dying far more from something that affects them much more commonly. Just as how homelessness has always primarily affected men and women have never cared about it until recently when it started to affect women a bit more and there started being more cases of homeless women, then women started to see this is another social issue. Things only become social issues when they affect women. Otherwise it doesn't matter how many men are dying, women see us as replaceable. That is because they view us without humanity. Which is why they are always trying to take away our sense of self and replace it with their sense of who they want us to be, which is just a common work horse to be used and discarded when no longer useful, and then replaced with another.

A man should never be made to feel like less of a man. A man is a man. Even if he doesn't pay for women. Even if he doesn't have a certain size penis. Even if he doesn't share the same values as a woman. And especially if he isn't willing to accept female abuse, he is still a man. It is not up for any woman to dictate what makes a man a man. Mother nature already did it by giving us our chromosomes, sex hormones and genitals. We are all men, and if any woman doesn't like it, it does not give her the right to try to make us feel like less of a man. Such a thing is dehumanizing, sociopathic, abusive, and goes against the idea of equality and that all people have the same human rights. And the only reason she would even attempt to do so is because of her own inferiority complex. These women can only feel better about themselves by making men feel worse about themselves. This is what they call female empowerment. This is what feminism has become. The misogyny of old was never so destructive towards women. In fact, while feminism today is largely about emasculating men, there is no word for doing the same thing to women. Efeminating or efemination are not real terms or concepts. Because besides a woman being told that she is acting unladylike for being rude (which she should, just as how men get told they are being ungentlemanly for doing so as well), such a thing does not exist. Men have never tried to make women feel like less of a woman, especially for doing so little as disagreeing with us or not conforming to our wishes.

I have even seen this tradition of emasculation extend to where men are supposed to be most Dominant in the most hardcore of ways. For it even occurs in the BDSM/kink community where Dominant men will be told that they are "not real Dom's" simply for not adhering to the female's image of how they want a Dom to be. Even if that image is misandristic and includes and hypocritical and includes the man catering to the female in ways she wouldn't for him. Women in the kink community have used the concept of consent and manipulated it to go from "you can't strike me without my permission, or do so harder than I like, etc" which is completely appropriate, to them saying things like "If you don't do this my way you are not a real Dom. Just as with women using the term "not a real man" in the vanilla social world, in kink culture they do the same things with Dom's and will tell a man he is not a real Dom if his style is not what they want/like. Women wish to be able to manipulate the sense of identity of even the most dominant men. And while there are certainly fake Dom's out there and there is nothing wrong with calling them out if they do something such as violating consent, this is not always or often the case. Breaking down a man/Dom's sense of self is not being used to call out fake predatory Dom's who might endanger submissives. It is being used to punish men for not being agreeable or conforming to women's feminist ideology. And this is so wrong I cannot even begin to describe it. And again, it is sexist, which is ironic that it is being done in the kink community which is supposed to be the opposite of sexist.

I remember my first encounter with these misandristic double standards (aka hypocrisy) in the sex ed and kink community. It was 8 years ago when I had a facebook group called "Sex positive polyamory". I had just posted two videos there on oral sex, one for men one for women. The one on cunnilingus had gotten half a million views. The one on fellatio had gotten 6,000. I asked why people thought that was. Some new age feminist who called herself a sex educator said, "Men need to learn to eat a woman out, women don't need to learn how to go down on a man". I asked her why that was, and she started talking about how men are sexual apes and will get hard and cum easily and any woman can do it and so women do not need to learn how to operate a penis because it is so simple. But on the other hand that women are complex delicate flowers and their vaginas are so complicated that men need to be taught how to use them properly. I told her she was being sexist against men and she started typing in caps telling me that she couldn't possibly be sexist against men because she teaches classes to women on how to pleasure men, and also there's no such thing as sexism against men, its not possible for a woman to be sexist against a man, because her gender studies teacher said so. I told her this was reverse sexism and she started ranting and raving with nothing but sexist psychobabble and I had to block her from the group.

        This was my first taste of misandry, and that was 8 years ago. Some would call it reverse sexism, but it's just sexism. But it is interesting that the messaging she was using was coming from the academic community of her university, which not only teaches third or fourth wave feminism that is really misandry under the guise of "gender studies", but it also that there is no such thing as misandry. And what is being taught about masculinity in university gender studies programs? Nothing, at least nothing that isn't emasculating to them. And ironically, not only is there such a thing as misandry, (otherwise there wouldn't be a word for it), but this is actually a perfect example of it. And denying that it exists is just further evidence of the misandry in the academic sex ed community, as well as feminisms attempt to dominate this world and make it gynocentric and focused only on women's issues and rights, and to wage a war on men and attempt to silence them when they speak out about having our own issues (most of which are caused by feminism), and to deny us having similar rights. But the fact is that sexism against men is more prevalent today than sexism against women. And feminism today is more about sexism against men than it is about fighting against sexism against women and earning them equality, since women have equality now, and sexism against women has waned so much that if that was feminisms main cause, there wouldn't be any need for feminism anymore. So to keep feminism going its cause has shifted away from equality and is now entirely onto misandry. And it's anti-male messaging is so mainstream that it is actually being taught in our universities, which seem to have turned into far left wing political indoctrination camps.

Since my first encounters with misandry in the Sex Ed community almost a decade ago I have seen this ideology grow more and more, and spread throughout other communities as well. Now most communities have become so gynocentric and feministic that misandry and double standards (hypocrisy) against men have become the norm and the general attitude in female/male relations is one of man hating. And not subtle man hating either. But overt man hating in which female on male hate speech is not even something that can be reported to moderators. This is a paradigm in which women are always right and men are always wrong (something we have heard before as a tradition in marriage), and in which even the slightest sexism towards women is not tolerated (even a man using his own words to explain himself, which is now very sexistly called "mansplaining"), but sexism towards men is not just acceptable but overwhelming. In fact I as a sex educator have been told by feminists that I have no right to teach female anatomy because I am a man and since I do not have a vagina I have no right to speak about one. Simply by trying to educate men on vaginas, because of the fact that they do not have them, I have been spoken to cruelly by feminists, saying that what I am saying is wrong, though it is not incorrect. When I ask them what I said that was incorrect, they simply repeat back to me what I said in their own synonymous words. The issue is not that I've said something incorrect, it is that I have used my own words and not theirs. What they call "mansplaining". But people are supposed to have a right to use their own words when talking and not have other people tell them exactly what to say and how to say it, that idea is fascist.

I at least speak in a manner that is polite and not intended to be rude or offensive, and it is quite wild when I am speaking in a way that is perfectly polite, and even politically correct, with a woman, who then reacts to something I say that she disagrees with by becoming extremely rude and offensive, and oftentimes beyond that, vicious. Men are taught to be polite and nice when talking to women, and to cater to them. Yet women being rude or offensive or even vicious towards men has become very common.   Women often speak to men in vicious and vitriolic ways and will attempt to break him down and be verbally abusive and destructive, when that man has literally done nothing to them to deserve it. Even though feminists have said that words can be a form of violence, because someone can be verbally abusive, that verbal abuse is actually a form of assault and violence, and so men should not talk to women any kind of way….but the same feminist rule does not apply to women talking to men. Women will speak to men in ways that feminists would call "Verbal Assault" if the genders were reversed, but when a woman does it to a man it is perfectly fine. The same thing goes with sexist language. Women use extremely sexist language towards men and not even see it as being sexist. However, women also can accuse men of being sexist towards them anytime they like, their definition for that has become so broad that it is almost all encompassing. It has become a card women want to play whenever they wish to justify starting a fight with a man and engaging in that kind of vicious/vitriolic verbal abuse towards him. Sexist language from men used to be exemplified by a man saying that women weren't men's equals, that women belonged in the kitchen, etc. Now of days a man can be called sexist for taking up too much space and find women screaming words at him that if a man were to say to a woman it would be called "hate speech".

This shows that after feminists fought for equality, there's no women out there who actually really want it. What they want is to be placed on a pedestal, and they believe men's place is groveling at their feet worshipping them while they berate them with the most atrocious degradation you could imagine. Could you imagine what would happen if men did this to women? But men are not allowed to talk down to women even in the slightest or else they will face social repercussions. In fact men can not use their voices in many of the ways that women can. Under this feminist ideology men do not even have the right to free speech. I can not even put out politically correct scientific information on female sex organ without feminists telling me that I have no right to talk about their genitals as a man and be accused of "mansplaining", and they will tell me that I am wrong (and in the most offensive and oppressive way that they possibly can) even when I have not actually said anything incorrect. Feminists and women in general seem to enjoy censoring us men and telling us what we can and cannot say, but they do not seem to care about being politically correct and non-sexist in their own language, because they know that they can get away with it as no authorities are going to moderate them and tell them not to use their voices how they want to. And that is another one of the first double standards/hypocrisy I am here to point out. For now after 8 years of suffering the sexist abuses I have suffered as a sex educator in that world, as well as others, I have finally decided to speak out against this misandry and hypocritical double standards against men.

I am going to be exposing some very dark truths about gender relations in the dating world at large, and more specifically in the communities that I have experienced them. And I am going to get a lot of hatred and backlash from man hating feminists because of it, but I feel I must stand up to them anyways. Because I am tired of being oppressed by these women who claim to be against oppression (another double standard). And since no one else is talking about these things, someone must speak out against their hypocrisy and unjust treatment of the male gender. I will start with the basics, and work my way up to the most outrageous. By the end of this article, whether you are a man or a woman, I am afraid you may have just shit your pants. And I apologize for that, but no one is speaking up about these things, and someone has to say something, and I guess that person has to be me. So without any further ado, let us begin.

2 – Emasculation & Feminization Of Men

The most basic form of misandry that is most common and often done casually and thus will often go unnoticed by the man, is Emasculation. Yet as men brush off instances of emasculation in their lives, there is a long term psychological castration going on. So lets take a moment to talk about the problem of emasculation.

Modern feminism and other aspects of society have been emasculating men for the past decades, and even going a step further than that and trying to masculinize women. This is not just a theory, it is evidenced by studies showing that testosterone levels have been slowly declining for some time. So in this chapter I am going to expose the ways in which society is emasculating men and trying to turn them into women so that we can fight against it.

- The removal of positive masculine male role models, which is done on two fronts, in real life, and in the media
- Removal of fathers from childrens lives through no fault divorce and the biased court system that only allows men to see their kids every other weekend, leaving the mother as the primary influence over the child, and mothers influence their boys not to be masculine but to be feminine. Most of the rest of the influences over the child are also female, the teachers, the people who run the daycare, the babysitters, etc. There are other male role models in real life which take the form of public figures, but none of these are teaching men how to be men, they are teaching success skills.

- Removal of positive masculine role models in media, in comedies the men are all stupid and subservient to women, in superhero movies the men might be muscular but they supplicate to women and exhibit more female traits than male traits, in action films the men are masculine but they are not positive role models.
- Boys and men are being taught that masculinity is toxic and the patriarchy is oppressive, and that the only way to be good is to renounce these things and become more feminine/feminist.
- Female influence over mens fashion, attempting to turn men into "metrosexuals", and even getting them to wear feminine clothing.
- The rise in sedentary careers is making men physically weak, docile, and low in testosterone.
- Nutrient rich foods such as fruits, vegetables and certain grains that were once peoples primary sources of nourishment have been replaced by estrogen and calorie rich foods lacking in nutrients, such as meat, dairy, processed foods, fast food, junk food, and sugary food. This has caused men to become low in T, high in estrogen, weak, fat and docile.
- Women have become the dominant gender and are controlling towards the men in their lives, which they don't do graciously and in a way that supports their strengths, but in emasculating ways which seeks to undermine their strengths, weaken them, and make them subservient.
- Women are constantly disrespecting men, shaming them, and doing other emasculating things with their language, all of which is actually programming mens brain to weaken them mentally and make them less manly
- When a man has emotional issues from all of this and seeks out therapy, the therapists will only emasculate

them further. The APA has issued a report declaring traditional masculinity is toxic. And therapists are always suggesting that their male clients adopt more feminine ways of thinking and acting, I know because I've been to plenty of them, both men and women. There was even a therapy workbook I bought that suggested that men imagine themselves as a scared little girl. So psychologists are literally attempting to get men to stop being masculine and feminize them.

- Feminism is trying to teach people that gender is just a social construct. The LGBTQ community is trying to turn men into women and women into men in the literal sense.

- Cell phones and social media are re-socializing men to cause them to communicate and act more like women. Broken English and miscommunication. Using emoji's and giffs instead of words. Taking excessive selfies and becoming obsessed with self image. And having a social life that is like that of a teenage girl.

- Female dating advice to men instructs them to be submissive to them, and many men have already been so influenced by women in their lives that they actually believe it

So now that you know how it is happening it is up to you to be able to recognize it whenever you see it happening and stand up against it in whatever ways you can. Resist being emasculated and feminized, fight back and be masculine! Now this is not to say that men cannot do anything that was traditionally thought of as a feminine oriented thing, like cooking and cleaning. This is not to say that a man shouldn't have feelings or express them. This is not to say that a man should be afraid of ever acting in a way that might be perceived as feminine, or having thoughts that he thinks aren't masculine. The answer is not to renounce anything that might be considered remotely feminine and just adopt a completely macho attitude. In fact as a masculine man you especially do not need to worry about these things. A masculine man can be in touch with the feminine side without it feminizing him, because he is masculine. So a manly man can prevent the feminine from emasculating and feminizing him, and can remain masculine and manly while being in touch with it.

Now that we have gone over emasculation, next lets talk about some of the even larger ways that gynocentric society is negatively impacting men, and actually feminizing them and turning them into women.

This may not come as news to you but testosterone levels have been on a steady decline for generations. And I know you all are familiar with the trans movement and some of the more overt and sexual ways that certain counter cultures like the LGBTQ community and feminism in general have feminized men, going as far as to put drag shows in schools and all that insanity. But I want to talk about some of the less obvious yet even more mainstream ways in which society is feminizing men and turning them into women.

The first thing I want to talk about that is turning men into more feminine like creatures psychologically speaking is social media and text messaging. Social media has conditioned men with this sort of female brand of narcissism that causes them to act more feminine. And I'm not just talking about the woke and mentally ill guys on tictok or anything like that. I'm talking about the narcissistic pretty boys who use Instagram the same exact ways as these thots and wanna be Instagram models that we men complain about. I'm talking about the shamelessly superficial and vapid guys

who act like social butterfy versions of NPC's, or worse,
catty bitchy little trolls, and either way they fit into those
same narcissistic sociopathic wannabe socialite mold that we
complain about in women.

But perhaps the worst of all are the men who are
actually successful and/or good looking and use social media
to broadcast these things to the world like a spoiled little
princess. Does anyone actually think that kind of insecure
feminine narcissism looks good on a man? Like I can't
believe that some of these men are actually really successful
on either social media or in real life because they seem to be
such fake fucking douche bags, who again, are acting like
narcissistic NPC's. The worst of the worst is probably the
guys who are into fitness. I'm into fitness and you'd only see
me post progress photo's 1 -2 times per year. Because you
won't really notice any observable changes if you were to
take pictures more frequently. It takes a lot of time for more
muscle to keep showing up, especially when you've been
doing it a while. But these guys who are trying to be fitness
influencers by posting this try hard bullshit multiple times a
day and trying to get validated for every fucking exercise
they do and every muscle every fucking day is a real shame.
This is why I can't be in the fitness industry I just can't stand
to see what's become of masculinity. And you have to admit
that men being overly focused on their appearance and
attractiveness is not only narcissistic, but its feminine, which
is why they end up looking like pretty boys. They aren't the
only ones though, these narcissistic trends on social media all
seem quite feminine to me, psychologically speaking.
There's this sense of deep insecurity and neediness for
validation like you would expect of a girlfriend. Posing for
pictures multiple times a day begging others to look at you
and like you…come on guys. Be a fucking man.

Then another thing that seems very feminine to me is
the way men have begun to talk, due to the fact that they are

doing most of their talking via text with their cell phones.
This has caused the quality and intelligence level and overall
length of communication to be diminished and minimized,
causing men to talk like teenage girls. This has not only
affected them via text message, but it has reprogrammed the
language processing center of the prefrontal cortext, retarding
it and causing it to become more feminine, like that of a
teenage girl. When grown men text me sounding like that
they are fucking done in my eyes. There's just no
communicating with someone like that who talks like an
immature little girl. Especially since a lot of them are quick
to get bitchy and even catty, or manipulative, displaying
behaviors I talk about when calling out toxic femininity in
women. It's like these guys just can't think and talk like a
mature adult man anymore. It's fucking pitiful. This is one
of the reasons men should just give up texting, or even cell
phones all together.

Another way that cell phones may be part of the
problem is that they are emitting radio waves when you have
it in your pocket next to your balls, so that's probably why
your testosterone is getting lowered. Another reason is your
shitty diet full of fatty sugary artificial processed foods.
Eating processed food with synthetic or artificial chemicals is
fucking up your hormones. And too much fat increases
estrogen making you feminine, fat weak and lethargic like a
big fucking bitch. And you know too much sugar causes
diabetes too. So this is why I make just about 100% of my
food from scratch. As an athlete I can't have anything
fucking up my hormones and giving me bitch tits. And over
the course of my life I've watched everyone get fattened up
like livestock. The average male is becoming a fat weak
feminine little baby due to his greasy disgusting diet.
Honestly as a cook most of the stuff people eat is fucking
pathetic to me. Like get some fucking standards what are you
a fucking dog? It's even called junk food, because everyone
knows that it is like eating trash, and yet they do it all day

every day anyway. I can't understand it. How about growing
the fuck up and making yourself some real god damn food
before you fucking kill yourself you big fat fucking baby.
Don't even get me started on how stupid I think people are
when it comes to eating. And its eating, the most basic of
things….like how the fuck can you be so bad at it?
Distinguishing good from bad food isn't that complicated.
Moving on…

Lets talk about one of the political and what feminists
call "systemic" ways that men are being turned into women.
It all started with the sexual revolution. What happened then
is that family structure changed from patriarchal nuclear to
matrilineal non-nuclear, with female familial power and
dominance and men becoming more like house husbands, or
in even more cases being estranged "baby daddy's", and in
either of these instances the father has less influence and even
presence in the childs life and development. This is
incredibly emasculating to men. I don't really think I have to
even tell you. And one aspect of that emasculation is the rise
of female players and supplicating simps and white nights
and other types of male pussy's by various names, who
basically let themselves get controlled by women like slaves
just for a taste of attention from her here and there. It's some
real weak pathetic bitch shit to see what a disease simping has
actually become.

Another emasculating and feminizing thing that has
gone along with the shift to a matriarchal family structure,
along with a political shift from patriarchy to matriarchy, is
that violence started being heavily discouraged in men.
Female violence, especially against men, became encouraged.
And men started being heavily discouraged and punished for
being violent, even when it seems justified, like in self
defense, even from a woman. It got so bad that they stopped
letting kids play rough sports in school and candy coated all
physical activities. Now my son tells me he has never played

certain sports in physical education class like dodgeball or wrestling. And one of the so called "phys ed" teachers I met recently was a morbidly obese woman. She was literally one of the heaviest women I've ever met, if not the heaviest. So drag queens in the schools isn't the only way our education system is used as social engineering in order to turn our sons into little girsl. And what do they eat at school? Hormone rich government cheese and basically food that is less than what prison inmates get. My son says it's like eating actual garbage. It's almost like they are fattening us all up on purpose, like livestock being lead to the slaughter.

As if that all wasn't enough, which it was, but just in case, feminism went on to really castrate us men like the livestock that we are when it convinced women that sexual proactivness from men is predatory and it started shaming men for showing any sexual interest or initiative with women they like, which was emasculating, but again as if it wasn't enough they then doubled down and started traumatizing men and ruining their lives for it, really cutting off our dicks and balls. Now if you want to let a girl know you are interested in her sexually you need to practically consult with a fucking lawyer first! Haha. So now men have become sexually passive like women, or even frigid like so many of them. I've certainly become very icy myself. And asexual. So I'm doing this little PSA here not because I think I'm better and haven't been effected by all of this. I've felt the effects of everything. I've felt the sexual shame and emasculation. I've felt the health problems from shitty American food I was fed in schools and even by my very own cunt of a mother too, who was a good old fashioned American narcissistic woman from the 50's who thought she knew how to be an ideal woman, and raise an ideal American boy, only to castrate me in every way she could just like all feminists do, starting as soon as I was born with having part of my actual dick cut off, why? Probably just so it would be easier for them to clean. They amputate part of our fucking manhood, just to make it

22

easier to clean. And somehow we don't see the red flags even when they are doing genital mutilation to male babies! What does it take for us men to stand against such human rights violations? Do they have to start giving boys vaginas at the hospital? Because that's probably what they'll do next.

However, most of our feminization is psychological. And one of the most upsetting ways they do it when they use manipulation tactics to try to get you to become more emotionally feminine, that is out of control. Which they do by for instance trying to provoke reactions out of you and then telling you that it is safe to open up and be emotionally vulnerable with them, and trying to make you feel like you can trust them only to then use whatever emotional information they get out of you against you by only using it to further trigger more emotional reactions and exploit your emotional weaknesses, as well as in greater manipulation plots such as with gaslighting campaigns which can adversely impact your mental health This kind of emotional manipulation a woman can make a man just as emotionally unstable and erratic as a female. And through gaslighting she can literally drive you insane so you'll feel emotionally just like a woman too! They will suck you in to their social webs of lies and deceit and trickery and mind games and drive you literally so crazy that you'll want to get a therapist just to mediate your arguments. But forget about getting a therapist because the whole field of psychotherapy is one of the ways that men are being feminized and something I'm going to be doing a deep dive into in the very near future so you can look out for that. But I'd just say when it comes to female drama and histrionics, forget about winning the argument, just get the hell away from her and stop letting her emotionally influence you! Even and especially if this is a woman who has made you feel like you love her, because that is their greatest mind game of all and if you let yourself fall for them you're fucked.

Even if you are like me and you don't date, even just being exposed to the modern female dominated workplace is subjecting yourself to female influence. Unfortunately if you work with women who are emasculating you there may be little you can do about it besides quit or go on strike. That's the last way that I want to mention that women can feminize men is through their corporate influence as we are seeing in woke culture. For women have taken over the workplace and have all the power and influence in it now. And I guess because a lot of people who work at these businesses are npc corporate drones they are having some success in changing the way men behave with women through things like mandatory sexual harassment and sensitivity trainings and other training programs that are really again forms of reprogramming.

So resist these forms of feminization any way and every way you can men. Go your own way and try not to let the matriarchy influence you. Alright so while I know I've used some strong words to try to get through to some of you, I'm not going to beat a dead horse, or try to break any of you down any more than this society already does. The point is to wake up to it and start resisting. Stop letting people treat you like a fucking bitch. Be a fucking man.

3 - Female Hypocrisy & Double Standards

One of the big ways that misandry is propagated is through the gynocentric paradigm of hypocrisy and double standards that women have against men, that basically says that women are always right and men are always wrong, and women can basically do anything they want but men can't do a lot of what women are allowed to. So here is a list of the biggest forms of female hypocrisy and sexist double standards I've observed as being commonplace in society.

A woman can hit a man but a man can't hit a woman, even in self defense when she is attacking him. A woman can beat on a man all she wants and not be thought of as an abuser, but if a man even does so much as pushes her away she can scream and call him an abuser and even call the police on him and get him charged with assault.

Men need to ask women's sexual consent but women don't have to ask men theirs. With a woman no means no, unless she actually means she wants you to keep trying. With a man, if he says no to a woman, she often sexually shames him.

Any mans sexual interest towards a woman can be construed as sexual harassment, but women are allowed to sexually harass and even assault men, and it isn't considered that

Women are allowed to have emotions and will say that men should too but then shame us for it when we do and say that we are being needy etc. When a woman cries she expects sympathy, even if she has just done something terribe. When a man cries he is bashed for it, even if something terrible happened to him.

Women say they want a good man who treats them well but when a man does they treat him badly and will then go hook up with some guy who doesn't treat them well, and then will call their friends sluts when they have random hookups

Women say they don't like drama and mind games but then engage in them every chance they get

Women say that men need to be attracted to them regardless of their physical appearance, and yet they are incredibly superficial when it comes to mens appearance and only go for the most attractive men out there.   Fat women can call themselves BBW's but there's no BBM's.   And women are even allowed to sexually objectify men based on a number of criteria (fitness, height, income,), and to objectify themselves, but men are not allowed to do anything remotely close to objectifying women (by focusing too much on her appearance).

Men and women have totally different professional standards. Women are hired less on merit and more on gender, whereas only the top performing men are hired.

Women expect men to make much more money than them (for them to be eligible for a relationship). Whereas the woman gets to choose any career she wants even if it doesn't pay well, or to be unemployed, and is not thought of as a failure or less than, as she would think of the man if he were to do the same.

Women often accuse men of being afraid of commitments, in order to guilt him into committing himself to her, which he is often willing to do FOR LIFE if she actually is putting in effort into being a good girlfriend, even though men's sexual instinct is to be polygamous. However it is actually women who have issues with commitment and attachment, and when they commit themselves to a man it is not for life it is just for while she feels like it. But if you tell her she is a commitment-phobe she will deny it and give you some BS about their feelings, which they are ruled by and will trump any commitments they've made.

In a couple a woman can try to make changes to a mans life, and if he doesn't make them he is not being a good partner, if he does, he is. However if a man tries to make changes to a woman's life he is "taking away her identity" and "oppressing her with his patriarchal control".

Any problems in the relationship are seen as the mans fault, even when they originate from the woman, she can find ways to blame him and their social circle will support her

When a man cheats on his female partner, it is because he is a pig. When a woman cheats on her male partner, it is because he was not supporting her sexual needs enough.

Male genital mutilation is normalized, female genital mutilation is a horrific human rights issue.

Men charged with a crime are criminals and deserve harsher punishments than women charged with the same crimes, who are seen as victims of the system and deserve leniency.

When a woman accuses a man of rape she is automatically believed, if a man accuses a woman of sexual assault he is laughed at. When a woman gets raped by a man it's a tragedy, when a young girl gets raped by a man, he is a pedophile and monster. These stories make the news and the man gets prosecuted harshly. When a woman rapes a young boy however she is not called a pedophile or child molester, it is not even called rape. It is called a sexual relationship, and she is given leniency.

If a man pokes a hole in a condom to get his girlfriend pregnant he can be charged with a crime. When a girl steals a mans sperm in this way or any number of others, it is not a crime, and he must pay her child support for 18 years.

Women say that they are strong and independent while exploiting men for money. Women say that they are as strong as men but don't want to take jobs that involve physical labor or have to compete against men in sports. Instead they say that this "equality" means that women should be getting into the highest paid positions in society, based upon gender, not merit.

A man who criticizes a woman is being negative (or worse), or if he criticizes women in general, he is being bigoted and sexist. If a woman criticizes a man or men, she is speaking her truth, and being brave for doing so.

If a man can't please a woman sexually it is his fault and he needs to learn how to do so. If a woman can't please a man it is his fault and he has "erectile dysfunction" and isn't a "real man".

If a woman wants a sex toy or to do something kinky, she is being sexually empowered, if a man does he is called a perv.

Claiming to be victims of the oppression of the patriarchy while they victimize and oppress men through their matriarchy Whenever a woman is disadvantaged in any way she can play the victim card, declaring to be a victim of circumstance and needing some sort of equity to elevate her above her victimhood. Anyone who tries to blame her for her situation and say that she is not a victim of circumstance but is actually a victim of her own bad choices, is then accused of victim blaming, which is unfair and oppressive to her. You cant, for instance, tell a woman who has been harassed or assaulted by a man that he may have done it because she was not being nice to him by leading him on and manipulating him until he reached a breaking point, she should assume no responsibility for her own victim hood. The man who wronged her is the one who should bear the full responsibility, even if she did play a role in the dynamic. However, when a man gets victimized do you think he can play either of these cards? Of course not, he won't be taken seriously and will be thought of as weak, especially if the person or people he claims to be victimizing him are female, then he will be laughed at and told to man up. He cannot try to accuse anyone of victim blaming him, for that is not how victim blaming works, the term is only meant to apply to when women are being victimized and blamed for it, not when they do it to men.

The Blame Game - when a man is in a relationship with a female he will be constantly blamed for things that he didn't do, and blamed for situations that he was not responsible for, and blamed for just about anything and everything. When the woman feels badly towards the man, it must be his fault. When the woman cheats on him, also his fault. When the woman hits him, certainly his fault, he must have deserved it. When the woman divorces him and takes half of his stuff and the kids leaving him heart broken, definitely his fault, after all, that's what he gets for being a man.

4 - Men Have It Far Harder Than Women Do

Women say that they have it harder than men. But they are actually just professional victims. They are indeed the weaker sex, and have learned to weaponized their weakness. They play the victim so that they can hide the power they have over us while making constant plays for more. Women have it so easy, they are like queens being carried by male slaves. Men have it much harder than women. In dating and female relations the man has to do all of the work, and incur almost all costs. In society men have to take all of the harder jobs. And women now get equal pay without being expected to do equal work. And they are even claiming to be so disempowered and oppressed by men that they should actually get even more than that, but guaranteed equal outcomes rather than just opportunity. Affirmative action has given women several legs up in society. And yet they still continue to complain that they have it so much worse than men. That they are so dominated by the patriarchy, when actually we live in a matriarchy and it is women dominating men.

Ask any woman who is claiming that men have it harder what evidence she has to support this. You two can of course compare experiences. But what would be more interesting would be to ask her if she has had any experiences as both a woman and a man? Of course not. So suggest to her that she try setting up a male dating profile just to see how women treat men in the online dating market. Watch her send out messages that she thinks sound nice enough, only to get no positive responses. That is if she even accepts the challenge. Most women will not because they do not want to be be proven wrong. But some women these days who are public figures or want to be social media influences ,are actually doing these experiments. There have been women who like to try to give guys dating advice and then will do this dating profile experiment only to be shown how wrong they are. But beyond that, there was even a feminist who tried dressing up as a man for 18 months and infiltrating the manosphere and mens support groups, and what she found shocked her. She discovered that it is so much harder to be a man and that men get treated so much worse than women. It shocked her, but any man listening to this probably isn't shocked. You are probably going wow I'm so glad that she realized that, but I'm not shocked that it happened, I mean, what else did you expect to happen? Her experience matched yours, because it took place in objective reality.

When a woman talks about male and female differences the way feminsts do without having this objective experience, she is speaking only from her subjective reality, which is a biased and limited perspective. And any woman who wants to talk like that without doing anything to empathize with men and understand what its actually like to be one, like the simple social experiment of creating a dating profile and sending out some messages, is being intentionally prejudiced against men. But there are no denying these facts. When a feminist publishes a book about her experiences living as a man and how wrong she was, other feminists cannot ignore this. There are even men becoming transgendered into women, sometimes not because of their sexual orientation or the gender that they feel they are, but because they want to have an easier better life, which they know they will as a woman.

Granted it is mostly due to the internal personality factors, but I have met one trans person who said they did it mainly because they knew they would have a better life, and they do have many privileges that they enjoy as a woman that they didn't as a man. And as for women who become transgendered into men? Well surprise surprise they are also reporting that life gets harder for them as a man. I know this because I have read articles written by female to male trans men which illustrated a number of ways that his life was now worse that he was a man in this world. These people report that society does not treat them as well as men, in spite of the fact that men are supposed to be the more privileged class, this is not what they experience. They are actually treated with suspicion and caution as if they are a potential threat. And I have even met a male to female trans person who said they mainly became a woman because they wanted to have a better life due to knowing that women were actually the privileged class, and that they did in fact get treated better and have it better as a woman.

There was even a feminist named Norah Vincent wished to document male privilege and patriarchal power and oppression by pretending to be a man for a year and a half. And what she discovered when she did this was that men are actually not at an advantage over women, but a disadvantage. In fact it was actually extremely emotionally difficult for her to live as a man. She not only saw how men suffered, but she actually experienced the pain and misery that they have to endure first hand for 18 whole months. She published a book about this called "Self Made Man" which she published in 2006 and there is also a documentary about her experiences which was featured on 20/20, and I encourage you to look up her story one way or another.

Norah states that while women are said to be the sweet ones, what she found out was that men are actually much kinder than women, and women are the meaner ones. She found men's communities much more accepting and supportive than women's communities, and that men were much less judgmental towards her than women are. She found that trying to live as a man in society is much harder, that she faced much more difficulties as a man, and felt much more alienated by society and disassociated. While people did believe she was a man she was also thought to be gay due to not being as masculine as society expects men to be, which is something that especially made dating hard. She went on many dates and found herself being rejected by every woman she met at singles bars, and written off by every woman she went on a date with almost instantly, almost as if she was being prejudicially discriminated against for not being manly enough. She even went to a retreat run by a mens rights activist, but after this she started to experience mental health problems due to her experiences as a man, which had worn her down emotionally.

Her experience was so disheartening and depressing that she checked herself into a mental hospital to be treated for anxiety and depression, and even the risk of suicide, which she felt she was in danger of committing. She needed so much mental health treatment for it that she spent a year in the clinic, writing her next book about those experiences. So unfortunately for her the feminist messages that she thought she was going to prove with this social experiment did not get proven, but the opposite was shown to be true. After returning to living as a woman she struggled to deal with the dark truths and harsh realities she had uncovered and to reconcile them with her feminist beliefs, and went down a downward spiral for many years.

Later, she attempted suicide at least twice unsuccessfully, and now I'd like to point out that when I began talking about her I said that there "WAS" a feminist named Nora Vincent, speaking of her in the past tense. This is because she recently did successfully commit suicide with assistance after so many years of being unable to cope with the social world as she now saw it after living as a man. She tried to go on for a long time but in the end she was unable to and she took her own life in a euthanasia clinic in Switzerland, dying on July 6 2022 at the age of 53. This story should be a real eye opener for all of us out there, however unfortunately it seems that it has gotten largely ignored by feminists, and women at large and that this woman who should be seen somewhat as a martyr for her causes is getting overlooked because of how she goes against the commonly accepted female narrative. And her status as a contrarian woman is probably what made her life continue to be hard after she went back to being a woman. For as she found out, women are meaner than men are. And as we men know, feminists are the meanest of all women.

Feminists like to talk about male privilege and how oppressed they are by the patriarchy, but it is really just a manipulation tactic. It is a victim card they are trying to play to make a power move. Women are the most privileged people on the planet, they live their lives in pedestals and in ivory towers. And men have it much harder than them, largely because of them and their status over us, as well as all the ways that feminism is constantly making these power plays, empowering themselves, and disempowering men. So when you hear one of these lies, speak up. Don't let them play these games anymore. And stop letting women make your life harder so that theirs can be even easier.

The Many Disadvantages of Being Male

1.) Men are much less likely to reproduce and have kids than women are.
2.) Men have to earn respect (and even then they are often not respected). Women are given respect without having to earn it, but just for being born female.
3.) Men are seldom allowed to be the victim when they are victimized (I know this from personal experience as someone who was assaulted on the job in a robbery, as well as assaulted by girlfriends)
4.) Men don't have the built-in support system that women have.
5.) Men are expected to suppress their emotions. Even the same people who say that men should be able to express their feelings will then punish them for doing so. Emotional men are vilified.
6.) Men work longer hours than women
7.) Men seldom receive the credit they are due. The patriarchy gets no credit for making life, easier, cleaner, healthier and safer through technology, education and medicine.
8.) Women receive more scholarships and educational opportunities and diplomas/degrees, and are now having their poor educational choices forgiven with the student loan forgiveness program.
9.) Welfare Programs for men are almost non-existent, they are there to serve women almost exclusively.
10.)   Feminism skews statistics and facts in its favor to make men look worse and women look better, or where necessary, to make

women look worse off and victims of circumstance, and men look better off…when oftentimes the facts are actually the other way around. Such as with domestic violence stats.

11.)   Male Domestic Violence shelters barely exist in spite of female on male domestic violence being more common. There is 1 homeless shelter exists for men vs over 2,000 for women.

12.)   Male success is dismissed to privilege rather than hard work.

13.)   Men are expected to be providers for women. Men can't marry for money but women can.

14.)   Male objectification is socially acceptable as Men are treated as success objects and status objects by women, while the objectification of women by men has been deemed unacceptable.

15.)   Women use men for their resources and this is socially acceptable, but a woman feeling used by a man for sex or anything else is not.

16.)   Man hating rhetoric is not seen as sexist but is socially acceptable.

17.)   Men are not naturally multi-orgasmic, women are. And the male orgasm is only a fraction as powerful as the females, specifically 1/8th.

18.)   Men cannot blame the government/patriarchy for their failures and bad choices but women can.

19.)   Men are always to blame and must take responsibility for anything that goes wrong in any situation with a woman.

20.)   Men are portrayed as bumbling idiots on TV Sitcoms controlled by a strong smart competent level headed woman, who is never wrong.

21.)   In TV commercials men are also portrayed as idiots, and any bad behavior or bad conditions (Allstate-Mayhem Man, Mucinex-Cold Character) are male characters and male voiced.

22.)   Violence against men in TV shows and TV commercials is portrayed as funny and harmless.

23.)   Male bashing and shaming is socially acceptable while female bashing and shaming is not.

24.)   Single mothers are deemed heroic in spite of the fact that they create more criminals and suicide victims and other problems with the children they raise. And the state doesn't allow men to become single parents, or even get equal custody.

25.)   Men marry women with debt, not the other way around.

26.)   Women are far more judgemental towards and rejecting of men than men are of women when it comes to dating, women can find something wrong with just about any man.

27.)   Men who are unemployed are considered losers, no such judgement for unemployed women.

28.)   Men are more likely to become homeless than women. There has never been any concern over this by women, or society at large. However as soon as the female homelessness rate started rising, it made the news and became a national issue.

29.) Men are expected to date down, called hypogamy. Women only date up, called Hypergamy.

30.) Men are expected to provide for women's children from a previous marriage, but no such obligation by women to provide for men's children from a previous marriage.

31.) Men's actions are constantly scrutinized for what may be perceived as being malicious against women, while contrarily women are given a free pass to behave maliciously against men.

32.) Male suicide is 5 times higher than women's, and there has never been any concern over this by women, or society at large. However as soon as the female suicide rate started rising, it made the news and became a national issue.

33.) Men are much more likely to be involuntarily celibate. For 80-95% of men out there, getting their sexual needs met is difficult and frustrating. Something no woman will ever understand for any woman can easily get a man who is more attractive than her to go to bed with her.

34.) Men seldom get paternity leave

35.) The police take the side of the woman in any situation involving both genders, even if it is the man who called them on the woman.

36.) Men are called predatory and rapey by feminists. And feminists say that men are the only ones who can rape. When a man gets raped or sexually assaulted, especially by a woman, it is ignored by them. And it will be by the justice system too if it was done by a female.

37.) Men cannot get "buyers remorse" after a sex act and accuse a woman of rape, but a woman can do this to a man quite easily, and can bring him up on charges even if it was consensual, and at the very least cause him a lot of problems, or at the most cause him to actually go to jail and get raped himself, for which of course he has no legal recourse or protection.

38.) Men have to tolerate female hypocrisy and double standards, which are normalized and socially acceptable.

39.) Men can't choose inequality when it is advantageous in one condition, then equality when it is advantageous in another (Traditional Gender Norm vs Modern Independent Woman), but women can.

40.) Men naturally die younger than women.

41.) Men's deaths make up the vast majority of work related deaths (because they do work that is harder on the body and Men are the majority in the most dangerous jobs (Armed Forces, Police, Fire Protection, Construction, Mining, Logging, etc.)

42.) Men's deaths during a war are far greater than women's (because they get drafted and women don't)

43.) Men are expendable, "Women and Children First"

44.) Men cannot opt out of war by getting pregnant in the armed forces.

45.) Men have no choice concerning a pregnancy.

46.) Men can be forced to be fathers.

47.) Men can be denied the right to fatherhood.

48.) Women can legally abandon children at Fire Stations, Police Stations or use Adoption, without the father having any say in it. Men can not do this.

49.) A father's emotional contribution to the family is considered less important than the mother's.

50.) Men's love of their children is not considered as strong as a mother's.

51.) Society has no concern for the lives of divorced men.

52.) Men are subjected to being "Baby Trapped" (Intentional Pregnancy by women)

53.) Men are subject to Paternity Fraud (Deceived by a woman to support child/children by other man/men)

54.) Men are made to pay child support and are treated as an endless supply of income for regardless of the condition of the economy and their employment. Child support can never be lessened even if the man loses income. And a man can actually be unconstitutionally jailed for non-payment.

55.) Men pay a disproportionate share of the tax burden.

56.) Men consume less in tax benefits than women (Welfare, WIC, Food Stamps, Medicaid, Social Security)

57.) Men pay taxes to support children they didn't create (Welfare, Food Stamps, Medicaid, etc.)

58.) Men are blamed for the poor choices that women make concerning the men women choose. When women date only bad boy alpha male assholes who are abusive and the friend zone the nice guys, they then start saying that all men are abusive assholes, and punishing all men for their mating choices.

59.)   Men are expected to adhere to outdated social traditions while feminism gives women more and more new freedoms and privileges.

60.)   Men are expected to initiate all contact with women they want to date.

61.)   Men are expected to pay for the dates.

62.)   Men are forced to finance organizations that are openly hostile to them i.e. Women's Studies, Affirmative Action, Universities and Colleges, etc.

63.)   Women can publicly insult and humiliate men, which has been proven to be a traumatic event, without any social condemnation.

64.)   Men who are unattractive, short, or fat get belittled by women. However women in these cases get empowered. Women who are unattractive get activism, women who are fat get to be called BBW's. The same woman who is unattractive and fat will actually belittle a man who is unattractive and fat, and say that she is worth more than him. If that man called himself a BBM and tried to empower himself with activism he would just get more public humiliation.

65.)   Sex is easily obtained for women, not for men because women generally do not find men attractive. And an OKcupid study where women rated mens attractiveness showed that women didn't find any men on the site to be the most attractive, and found the majority of them unattractive. A tinder study showed that what used to be the 80/20 rule is now more like the 95/5 rule. And yet even though the majority of men are marginalized in the sexual marketplace when they do not have sex they are shamed by women for it and called "incels". However when a woman feels marginalized in the sexual marketplace she calls it "problematic" "discrimination" and other such things which she needs activism, equality and empowerment for. Men who have been made into incels and sexually shamed by women do not get to do these things, lest they be further publicly humiliated by them.

66.)   Men have the burden of proof for consensual sex, no such requirement for women. Men are responsible for women's actions in sex (Drunk woman climbs into the front seat of a car and drives away and kills someone, she cannot say, "I was drunk; I didn't know what I was doing." The same drunk woman climbs into the back seat of the same car to have sex, later she can say, "I was drunk; I didn't know what I was doing." She is not responsible for her actions and the man is. The charge of Rape is based upon a woman's word.

67.)   A woman making false accusations against a man is not a criminal act.

68.)   Man's reputation can be easily ruined with no consequences to the woman (Mattress Girl, Columbia University)

69.)   Male circumcision is not seen as genital mutilation, even though that is what it is.

70.) Prostate Cancer receives little to no public attention vs Breast Cancer in society, even though men die from prostate cancer more. And there is Under-funding of research for male-specific medical disorders (prostate cancer, etc.)

71.) Father's rights are almost non-existent when compared to the mother's in a divorce.

72.) Men have the entire legal system stacked against them in legal dispute or crime involving a woman.

73.) Men receive longer sentences for the same crime. (For instance, a couple who was tried together for the same crime received different sentences, Lori Laughlin 2 months, her husband Mossimo Giannulli 5 months)

74.) Affirmative Action is Politically Correct Discrimination against White Males, based upon Sex and Race.)

75.) Men's Rights Activist meetings and forums at Universities are routinely protested by Feminists

76.) There are fewer men in college than women (2,200,000 more women than men in 2019)

77.) Double standard for violence. Woman hits a man - He gets laughed at. Man hits a woman, even in self defense, he goes to jail.

78.) Men are perceived as sexual predators, naturally violent or having criminal intent.

79.) Men don't get special treatment, entry or reduced prices as women do "Ladies Night" for drink specials, admission, etc. and special ladies only events, and special sales for women only.

80.) Separate but unequal bathrooms

81.)   Men's social injustices and issues are dismissed and ignored, male discrimination has been normalized and socially accepted.

82.)   Men have less rights and more responsibilities.

83.)   Women are loved by men unconditionally, men are only loved by women if they provide for them.

5 - Misandrist Standards Of Sex Appeal & Sexual Objectification

Women claim they are not sex objects and hate being treated as such. They claim that sexuality should not be objectified. Yet who is doing the objectifying? Not men. It is not as if men see women as mindless sex doll's. Rather the opposite, men are not superficial creatures. We appreciate beauty, but what we appreciate more is content of character and conversation. Things that women fail to provide because they are busy objectifying themselves and competing with other women to turn themselves into the ultimate sex object. Even after feminism, while women may claim they don't want to be treated as sex objects in one sentence, in the next sentence they treat themselves as not only sex objects but as prostitutes who's primary source of value is in their body, which must be earned or even bought. It is an old tradition for a woman to make a man "earn" sex with her through monetary acts such as paying for dates and gifts. And it is no secret that many women will pretend to be interested in a man and go on dates with him literally just to get free food, drinks and entertainment. Gold diggers and "sugar babies" are very prevalent in the online dating world, as are cam girls who will lure men in with a dating app profile only to seduce them into paying for screen time with them. All of these are examples of women treating themselves not just like sex objects, but prostitutes.

Whether a woman is making a man earn sex by paying for dates and buying her gifts, or she is asking for him to take care of some of her bills in exchange for spending time with her, it is prostitution, and the most sexually objectifying act there is, which is something not done to women by men, but done by women to themselves. The only difference between these examples and outright prostitution as done in a brothel is that these examples are less honest and more manipulative, which actually makes them worse. These forms of prostitution are especially prevalent in the online dating community where the women expect men to compete for their attention and earn their affections as if it were an episode of the bachelorette.

There are also innumerable sex workers using dating profiles to scam men into paying them for their attention. And then there are the cam models and porno girls who make it seem like they are looking for partners but are really just trying to get men onto their onlyfans page to make them pay to watch them masturbate. And there are even these new types of sex workers who do not even consider themselves sex workers, but call themselves "sugar babies", who pose as mock girlfriends and expect to be compensated for the dates they go on with men. But worst of all there are the financial predators, these are women who are con artists called gold diggers who are looking to get a man to invest in them long term, or there are even women who do not do this covertly, but obviously, called "Financial Dominatrixes". But no matter what they are called or how they do it, there is a significant amount of the female population on dating websites who are looking to get paid directly for their sex appeal without even offering anything in return. And there are even more of these in the world outside of dating sites as well. So if women are not sex objects, why do they treat themselves as such? And not just as objects, but often worse, as prostitutes?

There's much more to it though. Women do not only objectify themselves, they objectify men as well. And they actually do this even more than they objectify themselves, or

48

were ever objectified by men before feminism. They treat
men as not only sex objects, but status objects, and monetary
objects. They force men to compete for them in order to
objectify the highest status man to give their attention to,
which they will do based solely on looks, status and ability to
provide, not on content of character or conversation as men
evaluate women based upon. And this is because actuality
women are the superficial ones, not men. It is ironic because
women are always claiming to not be superficial and to
dislike it when men view them in a superficial way. But just
as how women oftentimes do not want what they say they
want, you will find that they oftentimes use reverse
psychology to gaslight men into being fooled about their
hypocrisy.

However it is very hard to fool us men when you
show us exactly how you are with your dating. And women
care more about looks than men do, and they do not care
about character, but instead status and money, and this is
because they are extremely shallow superficial characters.
And it is a very hypocritical double standard as well, because
they do not want men to be the same way, not even a little.
This is why it is acceptable for a woman to ask a man how
tall he is, but not for a man to ask a woman how much she
weighs. It is acceptable for a woman to ask a man how much
money he makes, but not for a man to ask a woman how old
she is. And in the kink community it is even acceptable for a
woman to ask a man how large his penis is, but have you ever
heard of a man asking a woman how tight her vagina is? No,
because it wouldn't be appropriate.

Women are way more judgmental towards men's
appearance than men are towards women. Because women
are so much more superficial than men the standard of beauty
is way higher for men than it is for women, in fact it is
impossibly high. According to studies done on the swiping
patterns on tinder years ago, women in general only find the

top 15% of men attractive enough to give a chance in dating. This means that in women's eyes, 85% of men are considered below average looking. Now think about that for a second. If you understand the basics of statistics, you would understand that this is completely illogical. An average is something that in this case should occur close to 50%, now it would be different depending on range of the amount of options being tested (if you were testing 10 different things, then your most average number would be lower), but here people were being tested with a binary yes or no method. So the average should have been close to 50%. If the female reality was rational, fair and realistic the results should have been close to 50/50 on each side. So 85% is a number far above the average, and yet that is what they are rating as below the average. There is no way in a logical universe that 85% of men can be considered below average looking. But women now view the average man as being below average.

Though that was years ago, during the end of the third wave of feminism. This was tested again more recently now with the fourth wave of feminism influencing female culture, and women's standards have gotten even more impossible. The new results are that women only find 4.5% of men to be attractive/above average. So that leaves 95.5% of men being considered below average or unattractive to women! That number is not an average, it is a vast majority! It is an overwhelming and insanely large number! This is what I mean when I say that women's standards are impossibly high. Because they are overtly judgmental towards men. While men in general find the majority of women attractive enough to give a chance. And our numbers are much more rational. With men recently rating 61.9% of women attractive/above average. This is a number that makes sense and seems natural. And this is because men are not predisposed to be so superficial as to judge and qualify or disqualify a person solely based on appearance alone, and when we are made to evaluate women based on appearance alone, we are not going to be objectifyingly judgmental about it and go calling the vast majority of women unattractive. That type of objectification is something only women do.

However these studies get even more interesting when you make them more specific and non-binary. A more in depth study was done on okcupid in which people could rate each other across a 7 point spectrum from least attractive to most attractive, it showed just how realistic men's standards are, and how women's impossibly superficial standards to be much worse. Men's ratings of women appeared as a bell curve, with 6% getting a 1 for the least attractive, 16% getting a 2, 18% getting a 3, 20% getting a 4 for being average or moderately attractive, 19% getting a 5, 15% getting a 6 and 6% getting a 7 for the most attractive. This sounds quite reasonable and natural doesn't it? Yet women's standards were shown to be extremely judgmental and negative towards men. With 27% getting a 1 for the least attractive, 31% getting a 2, 23% getting a 3, and 12% getting a 4 for being average or moderately attractive, 5% got a 5, and 2% got a 6. What about the 7's you ask? There were none. That's right, NONE! 0% of men scored a 7.

Let me reiterate this to you differently. On the female scale, 92% of men are considered moderately attractive or below attractive, but of that 92%, a whole whopping 81% of them are considered below average and not even moderately attractive. Again, 81% cannot possibly be BELOW the average. If anything 81% should be the average. And that is not even including the ones they rated as moderately attractive, which was only 12%. 12% cannot be the average! Now this test was not binary, you had 7 different options. So the most average would not have tested around 50%. It should have been 20% like it was with the men's even bell curve. But 12% is far below what the average should have tested at. And even if you included the 3's and 5's in calculating the average, which if this was close to an even bell curve should have landed you at 50%, you only get 40%, (unlike the men's bell curve where the middle three add up to 57%). And with the female data only 7% of men are rated as above average, and that is only in the first two categories, with no men scoring in the highest most attractive one.

If women consider 81% of men to be unattractive, 12% to be average, and 7 percent to be attractive, that should tell you just how superficial and judgmental they are about men's looks and how impossibly high and irrational their standards are. Now imagine what their response would be if they heard that men were judging them so harshly. They would accuse us of objectifying them, and would complain about the impossible standards of beauty imposed upon them. When us men are the ones having that very thing done to us, and righteously so. It is part of the feminist girl power narrative for women to have high standards, standards so high that basically no man could ever reach them, because it's not really about having standards, its really just man hating sexism. And if you were to call it a standard, you could only really call it a double standard. It's a hypocrisy. This shows a great impairment in female logic and reason, and the ability to judge and evaluate things reasonably and fairly, which is exactly where double standards come from.

There is further irony in online dating as well. When a woman matches with a man, if she wants to have a conversation the chances are that he will have one with her, and if she wants to meet in person the chances are good of that, and chances are also good that he will look exactly like he did in his pictures. However when a man matches with a woman the chances are good that she will not communicate with him hardly at all, because she will only be using that dating app for validation, not for connections. So chances are even worse that she will meet up with him for a date (which is what the app is supposed to be for). And when a man does meet a woman, she never looks like she does in her pictures. In fact most women are so superficial that they have mastered the art at manipulating their appearance, not just through using makeup, but through taking pictures of themselves at just the right angles to make themselves look better, and then editing the photos to make themselves look even better than that. And women will often be using photos of them when they were younger, by 5 years or more. I recently signed onto a dating app to find women that I had seen there almost a decade prior using the same pictures of themselves from then. And it is not out of the ordinary for a man to schedule a date with a woman and have her be much more overweight than she was in her pictures as well.

For a gender that is so superficial towards men and demanding of the best looks, at least we show our real faces on dating apps and you can expect to get what you see. You'd think that if they were going to have such high standards they would have higher standards for themselves and would not be pretending to stay young and hot online only to show up being older and fatter than their pictures indicated, all while demanding that we be over 6 feet tall and jacked. But this is growing less and less common as women are less and less prone to meet up as well probably for fear of being exposed for the fakes that they are, and also because they are now mainly using dating apps for validation from men and not real dating, so you are most likely to get ghosted as a man before a woman will meet up with you.

In the kink community, which is entirely centered around sexuality, the objectification of men is even worse. Women think that we are all here just to be used to fulfill their sexual fantasies and that they can message us instantaneously to do so. Even if it says not to do that in your profile, because they don't even bother reading your profile since they do not care about who you are as a person. They only care about what you look like and how they can use you to fulfill their sexual desires. I get messages all the time from women on kinky dating sites trying to treat me like some sort of "insta-Dom" to fulfill their fantasies and even going right into role play calling me sexual names I did not ask to be called (when women have made it known to men that they do not even want to be called things like "hun" anymore by men they don't know), and it even says not to do this in my profile and some of these women claim to have read it and yet still do it anyways. And trying to have a real conversation with women and develop a real relationship will mean getting ghosted because they are only there to use and objectify men to fulfill their desires, nothing more.

When I do one of my social experiments (which as a social scientist I do a lot of), and put up a female profile on a dating site I never see any messages like these, instead men message her acting polite and trying to have a nice conversation. So it seems that the cold hard truth is that men come to online dating and the kink community to make connections, and women do so to use their sex appeal for narcissistic validation, and if they are going to interact with men at all, to do so only to dehumanize and use them as sex objects.

Women are more than just superficial and shallow about men's looks, they judge and accept or reject men based largely on status and monetary value as well. They don't just objectify us based on our sex appeal, but they objectify us by treating us like status and monetary objects too. Something that has never happened to women. But women do this to us because they do not see us as humans, they see us as objects, things to be used. And they have these objectifying high standards because they are hypergamous. This means that they date up in attractiveness and status and monetary value. This is why it is common to see a rich man with a poor woman, but you would never see a rich woman with a poor man. It is also common to see a more attractive man with a less attractive woman, but almost unheard of to see the reverse. Because men just want a girl who looks healthy and takes care of herself in the looks department, but more importantly is a nice good person who seems like girlfriend material. But conversely women now want only the tallest, most muscular, most attractive of men, and not only that but the richest as well. And that is ALL women, even if they themselves are not as fit and attractive, even women who do not value their own health and fitness feel they deserve a man who is devoted to his.

Ever notice how overweight women are now called Big Beautiful Women (BBW's), but overweight men are still just called fat? Why are overweight women being called beautiful and overweight men are not? And these overweight women do not date men who are overweight too, they are looking for men who are fit as well. Why is that? Because women do not care about body positivity in general (for both sexes), just as how they don't care about equality. It is another hypocritical double standard. That women are allowed to have impossibly high and superficial standards that objectify men. Men however are not even allowed to prefer that women be healthy and fit or somewhat attractive, or even show that they evaluate women on such things at all, otherwise they will be accused of being sexist, objectifying them, not being "body positive" enough and not accepting women for who they are. When those accusations are really just projections of what women do to men, and it shows that it is a Double Standard (hypocrisy) because they do not like it when we evaluate them and have standards, yet they do it to us in the most dehumanizing way.

Yet women do not have to accept a man for who he is, even if he is below average looking, and so is she, she will think that she deserves someone above average looking. Even an average looking guy who is a definitively upstanding male role model will not be valued by women if he does not meet their high physical standards of attractiveness. In fact women are allowed to treat men as nothing but sex objects, it is socially acceptable because of the fact that they lie in their social narratives and say what they are really looking for is a just a good guy, but their actions say that they do not care at all about a mans character, or if he is a good person at all. Studies of the swiping patterns on tinder show that men who are average looking but seem like good characters based on their profile get largely rejected and will get very few matches except from the lowest tier women, while women will overwhelmingly swipe right on a good looking guys, in spite of what their profile says about them. In fact tests have shown that even if the mans profile says horrible things about him, like that he is a criminal, for as long as he is good looking women at large will swipe right on him. And women say that they aren't superficial and just want a good guy. That is the opposite of the truth, it is hypocrisy, and they only say that because they have to deny the truth for their public image since would make them sound like the terribly amoral and shallow creatures that they are.

Due to the body positivity movement (which is a women's movement that includes all female bodies and excludes all male bodies) even the women out there who have absolutely no care or respect for their bodies and abuse it treating it like a garbage dump can now demand that the highest tier men show their bodies respect and treat them as if they are beautiful. In fact they feel entitled to mate with these men. And as for the men that look like male versions of themselves? They wouldn't give them the time of day. No woman would. In fact no man below the 15 percentile is getting much any attention from women, even the lowest tier ones. Because women are that shallow and superficial. Not even a good looking but basically average man with great character can expect to get a mate anymore except on rare occasion. Even with his equal, because there is no equality among men and women in the dating marketplace, only double standards). All women now think that they deserve to be with the best looking most high status guys.

There is no body positivity movement for men as there is for women and men who are less than that 15 percentile get physically shamed by others constantly with no support from any sort of social causes or political movement like women have. Women's bodies in general are celebrated and they are told that "all of their bodies are beautiful" and that they don't have to change but just accept themselves the way that they are. A woman can show herself in revealing or skimpy clothing and get nothing but praise and admiration for it, while a man cannot. If a man shows his body and is not in peak physical condition he is going to get shamed for it. And even if a man is in peak physical condition he will never get the amount of praise and admiration that even average looking women will get. Society caters to women, especially attractive ones, and makes sure they are taken care of in any situation, whereas the cards are stacked against men. Women can be successful in life based off of beauty alone and not have to put in much work to get paid. Men however have a very difficult career path to try and be successful, especially when competing with any attractive women who will be favored in the workplace based on their appearance alone.

If a woman wants to have a healthy active sex life all she has to do is declare her gender and willingness and she will be able to have her sexual needs met consistently without having to put in any real effort what so ever because the men will do all of it, even if a woman is completely passive the entire time (and feminists say that they reject the passive female gender role, yet they maintain it in dating). However if a man wants to he has to get into his top physical condition, overcome social anxiety and the intimidation of talking to attractive women and start doing so constantly, pursue countless women and be subjected to all manner of tests, trials and tribulations by them…Including what are called "shit tests" in which a woman will actually treat a man like shit (and say/do things to him that would never be acceptable the other way around) in order to test his strength)….And then if he passes these tests he will have to deal with constant flaking and other rude and inconsiderate behavior. Not to mention self-entitlement and the expectation that the man is also going to be paying for her and treating her like a queen without getting anything in return...and all for what? To be able to have sex once in a while, in which he will more often than not have to settle for a woman that is below himself in attractiveness, and in which he is doing all of the work and the woman is playing an entirely passive role and not making any effort, just like she does on dates and will continue to throughout the entire relationship.

Even though the reality is that women, especially attractive ones, are the most privileged on the planet, feminists still talk about male privilege and all the sexism and sexual objectification and unfair beauty standards put onto women by men, and how sexist this patriarchal society is towards them and how hard they have it and how easy it is for men, based upon our gender alone. This is all a big fat terrible lie they tell us as part of their reverse psychology just to hide the fact that they are actually the one's with the privilege, and we are the ones with sexism against us. And women are the ones who use sexual objectification and create unfair standards in the sexual marketplace. And women are far more sexist against men than men have ever been towards them.   And if you want to debate this, try a little social experiment that I have done myself. Take some pictures of an average looking guy, someone who is not very attractive but certainly not unattractive, and create a dating profile for him. Make him out in his profile to be a great guy, upper middle class (not rich but well off, and classy) the type of guy that would be relationship material.

Now message as many attractive women on the site who seem like they could be a good girl as you can, with whatever line you think would start a good conversation with them. Because this is a social experiment you need a good sample size, so copy and paste this message to at least 100 profiles to start. And see what you come back with. This is something that every woman should do, especially before talking about male privilege and how easy they think men have it, or saying anything about men's dating issues. But whenever a woman will say such things to me I will always suggest she do said experiment. But they never do because it's so much easier to be prejudicial and pass negative judgements on men and accuse them of male privilege than it is to try to understand them and find out how hard they actually have it.

I on the other hand do know what it is like for you as a woman because I have seen the inboxes of the women I have dated, and not only that but since I am a sex educator I have taken it upon myself to do social experiments where I make female dating profiles for women myself to see what it's like for them. This was important to me as an educator so that when I spoke about what it's like for women in dating I was not doing it from an ignorant prejudicial standpoint. And this isn't just important as an educator. But for anyone who wants to be able to relate to the opposite sex in a healthy way and connect with them in dating you must try to understand what it is like to be them, for without understanding there is no empathy, and without empathy there is no connection, and that is why most people these days are not forming relationships. So give this a try, I promise it will be good for you.

Of course, I already know exactly what you will experience as a man, so you do not have to tell me. And I am not just saying that because I am a man who has had my own experiences. I have also heard about the experiences of women who have done this social experiment themselves, and it was very enlightening and inspiring to them. So I hope you can enlighten and inspire yourself with it as well.   And luckily for you it is just an experiment and you are not actually dating as this man you have created a profile of, so you get to experience it and then leave it behind, unlike us men who do not. But think of it as a role play for a moment and imagine what it would feel like to actually have to try to date as this average but good man, facing these kinds of rejections day in and day out. Thinking about it as a sensitive woman who doesn't ever have to deal with rejection, it's just about enough to make you want to kill yourself at times huh? Now you are starting to get a sense of how we feel and why the male suicide rates are so high. Luckily for us external validation means a lot less to us than it does to women who seem to feed off of it.

The problem is that women really don't have to thinknabout what it's like to be a man. We can try to tell them but they can just go back to your cushy female lives without really even considering what we've said. In fact any time a woman even feels bad about herself she can just go online and expect to share her feelings and get emotional support and validation (as opposed to the harsh rejections we experience as men). Women never have to face any harsh rejections, only rejections that are so polite that they don't feel bad. This is just one of the female privileges you'd get to enjoy as a woman. Something they most certainly take for granted and don't even realize what a privilege it is.

Female privilege is a very real thing. Though you may not have heard the term before, it not only exists but it is far greater than whatever you think "male privilege" is based on whatever propaganda the feminazi's have been feeding you. But don't take my word for it, google it. Just skim through all those pages of lists of different female privileges that men don't enjoy, and you have probably been taking for granted this whole time. Which brings me to my next double standard, which is just another one of the female privileges you get to enjoy, and that is the level of respect that they get automatically from men just for being female, and without even having to give it in return.

6 - The Double Standards In Manners & Respect

Should a woman decide she's no longer going to play into the passive female gender role that women have the privilege of playing, and not just wait for the men to make the first move, but actually put in some effort, (which is rare), she can simply go out and start chatting up men and she will not have to suffer any sort of rejection, unless the man she is chatting up is already in monogamous relationship, and even then it will be a very nice rejection compared to the way women reject the men who try to chat them up. Even the lower tier women will find men receiving them politely and probably have most of them give her a chance, men on the other hand will have an extremely opposite experience in trying to date women, unless of course they are in that top 15 percentile. But you see women do not just objectify men with their superficial attraction towards the top tier men in spite of their lack of character, or having a bad one. If you thought that was bad, it actually gets far worse.

Women objectify men even worse with their inhumane and even dehumanizing treatment of the men they find unattractive who try to date them. The fact is that an average looking man cannot date without having to deal with seriously harsh rejections. And while many women are polite about it, many are not at all, but even when the man is being polite with them, they will be extremely rude and uncalled for, or sometimes unconscionably harsh and malicious. Women tend to treat men as though we do not have feelings, or that our feelings do not matter to them.

Being lead on with lies and then ghosted is of course very common these days, something that women complain about not liking when those alpha male bad boys in the 15%

do to them, but then they turn around and do it to all of the other guys. And then equally common are the women who are insulted that a less than stellar looking guy would even work up the confidence to ask her out and think she might say yes to him, who feels it necessary to break him down just for trying with her with the cruelest comments she could possibly think of to lower his self esteem as much as possible, comments like "tell your parents they shouldn't have procreated because you are the ugliest man I've ever seen" are just one example (verbatim) from my own dating on a vanilla dating website, and I am actually considered above average, so I can just imagine what below average men have to deal with. Or the last message I just got on a dating site from a girl who I didn't even solicit, who said "your profile made my vagina drier than the sahara desert and girls should run far away from you." That's just from a woman who simply didn't like my profile, which doesn't have anything offensive or hateful in it. That is the way women feel is appropriate to speak to someone they don't like the personality of or who says something they disagree with.

Then there are the women who choose to publicly humiliate and shame a man for asking them out. Every man who has made a serious effort at dating has had to deal with public humiliation and shaming by women, which according to psychology is an extremely traumatic experience that deeply changes a person, which women do simply out of narcissism and leaves a man needing therapy (I literally had to get therapy for a public humiliation and shaming that I suffered once). Some women are even known to take this public shaming a step further and report said man to an authority of some sort for harassment and get him in trouble, like the time I had a female employee at the museum who I had made small talk with (and not even asked out or flirted with or done anything to suggest I was interested), call security on me in front of my son. Or worse, they may even recruit a large alpha male friend of theirs to intimidate or threaten him.

Of course, the more extreme the scenario the more of an outlier it is, but they are common enough that any man who has put himself out there enough will encounter them from time to time. I know, because all of these happen to me, and not just once each, but from time to time. And never have I ever done anything to elicit that kind of response from a woman. I'm not approaching them sexually harassing them or anything of that nature. I'm trying to make a connection, I want her to like me, so of course I am being polite and friendly. And I'm not the only man that these things happen to, I've talked to other men who have had similar occurrences as well. This kind of excessive cruelty towards a man who has had to overcome the extreme nervousness and anxiety that anyone feels when approaching someone they are attracted to to ask them out, something that women barely ever have the courage to do themselves, and who speaks to her in a very socially appropriate and polite manner that should elicit no ill will in return, shows an extreme lack of humanity and sadistic psychopathic personality. And again, these are not isolated incidences here or there. They are patterns. These all are.

The fact is that a large portion of women out there feel the need to treat men out there in the dating pool in a completely dehumanizing manner, simply because they are not attracted to them. Now when the roles are reversed and on the rare occasion that a woman ever decides to be less passive and more pro-social and try to meet guys and ask them out, how often do you think she will experience a harsh rejection? Not even as harsh as some of the ones that I have illustrated. But just a little harsh. Or extremely rude. Even if she is extremely unattractive....I'll give you a hint, it's a very low number. Probably lower than what you are thinking. And even lower than the new number you are thinking of.

Think of the lowest number you can possibly think of. If your answer is never, or almost never, that is the correct answer. Men simply do not punish women for being social and giving them attention. And they certainly would never do so as harshly as women do to men, again, just for being social. We are just not that cruel and inhumane towards women like women are towards men. Because we recognize that women are human beings with feelings and should be treated with respect, just like we would like to be treated.

A lot of women do not recognize men's feelings, or even recognize their humanity or need for common human decency and respect. In fact their ability to cut a man down makes them feel empowered. This is due to narcissism. They view themselves as queens and men like slaves, hence their inhumane treatment of us. Women love to talk about how they know their worth and won't settle for less, or even how they are Queens or Goddesses. But this is not based upon their content of character. It is pure narcissism, it has nothing to back it up but a superiority complex. If you ask them what makes them have such high value, or ask them anything about who they are as a person, they won't be able to tell you, and may even start acting psychotic from being questioned and made to think about it. It seems that they do not know the difference between having a strong personal identity and high self esteem, and just plain narcissism. It seems feminism failed to teach women the difference.

I myself was raised to be an old fashioned gentleman by a mother who was a socialite (and a first wave feminist) and taught be extremely polite and respectful in all of my social interactions, especially with women. But surprisingly I somehow also end up getting disrespected by women who I am polite with. And usually it is after telling them that I prefer not to be spoken to in such a way or called a certain name, and that it does not feel the way I wish to be respected as a man. Those simple words which I use verbatim anytime someone says something that I feel isn't respectful are enough to make a narcissistic woman start lashing out at me and saying things that are way further over the line. When you are dealing with people who have anti-social tendencies, you cannot expect them to treat you with respect even when you are acting respectful towards them and respectable. But we live in an antisocial age these days, and lots of people have anti-social tendencies, especially with text based communication. But social technology affects women far more than it does men. And far more negatively.

These days a man simply cannot expect to communicate constructively with a woman via textual communication and expect to have a nice civil conversation. He can try to start an in depth conversation and be met with one word answers. He can be polite with her and expect her to be rude. This is the new standard of behavior. And when you get a woman in person and try to have a conversation with her verbally, she will still be responding to you with short, curt, and even rude answers…because she will still be giving most of her attention to her phone. If you try to politely tell her that she has spoken to you in a way that is not the way in which you feel you ought to be respected as a man and would appreciate it if she spoke to you differently, you can expect her to become more rude and inappropriate than before and to lash out at you just for suggesting she ought to change her language. And she feels as though she can get away with doing this because she doesn't need to pay you any mind when she has cultivated a following of a multitude of other men on fetlife and her other dating and social media apps that she has gotten supplicating to her by posting sexual innuendos, images and videos.

Women demand respect from men in all of the most minute of ways, but they do not offer it in even the most basic ways. They have become rude and unable to hold civil discussions with men because they are addicted to their phones, which like any addiction has negative mental health implications and causes them to exhibit the same types of bad behaviors any addict does. So if you try to get between a woman and her phone and point out that she is not being polite and should try to have a conversation with you since she came to spend time with you in person (especially if it is a date), she will become indignant and blatantly rude. How dare you tell her what to do with her attention! Because she is an addict, and attention is her drug. And in the kink community on kinky sites and other forms of social media that have sexual sides to them, this type of addiction is a sexual addiction. But it is not an addiction to the act of sex, but sexual validation. And that sexual validation is oftentimes what a woman is feeding off of when she is giving a man any kind of sexual attention. He may think that she is actually interested in him as a person, but in fact she is only interested in him as a source of narcissistic supply.

Women are not on these apps to engage in conversations, but to get validation for their sexuality and beauty as sex objects. So don't worry men, she's not ignoring your in depth conversation to have an in depth conversation with someone else. She's just scrolling through notifications and comments from people telling her how nice the selfies she has been posting at least once an hour are. And if she is part of the kink community you know that those notifications are going to be much more sexually explicit, because they are most likely in response to her posting pictures of her breasts and vagina. This gives new meaning to the phrase "attention whore", since these women are literally whoring out pictures of their private body parts and other sexually explicit imagery for attention and validation from men. So when you are a man trying to have an in depth conversation with a woman to get to know each other for the purposes of a healthy relationship, and while you act like a gentleman she cannot even bother to treat you with respect or be polite because she is too busy fishing for external sexual validation from an infinite number of men on social media….what do you think that means exactly? It means that she belongs to the streets. And you cannot expect a woman who belongs to the streets to treat you with respect, even when you give it to her, because that is just not the language of the streets. A woman like this will never belong to any man, she can't even be bothered to have a nice conversation with a well mannered well meaning gentleman. It is just like the old aphorism "you can't turn a whore into a housewife".

Even if she claims to be a "good girl" who is looking for a Gentleman, chances are she really is not and is just overselling herself to you. And that is why you may act like a Gentleman and abide by the protocols of the social etiquette, only to feel like you can't communicate with her because she is curt at best and rude at worst, and cannot even tell you about what she is looking for, wants from a man or consents to, because she doesn't even know what she wants. You will end up arguing with her because she expect you to read her mind when she doesn't even seem to know her own mind, and in order to get you to be more compliant the term "Gentleman" will start to arise again, only now it will be her telling you that you aren't a real one unless you do as she says. It turns out that even the girls who seem like "good girls" are not so innocent underneath that façade, but are also prone to malevolence and misandry, and will try to break down your identity to gain compliance like all the others. In fact most girls who say that they are looking for a Gentleman are doing so because they know that men who fancy themselves put in more effort to cater to and provide for the women they are dating. So most of the girls who call themselves "good girls" are actually just greater users and manipulators of men and are looking to try to exploit even more special treatment and provisions out of him than others might.

You may think that you are dating a nice, sweet, innocent girl who you have a romantic connection with because you are going through all the social niceties of courtship with her and have had some moments together that seemed very special…but the reality is that she does not feel the same towards you. If she does think that she feels any kind of emotional connection towards you, it is not a real one, it is just a label she is putting on the pleasant feelings that are caused by you doing things for her. The fact of the matter is there is little chance of her continuing to even give you the time of day if she couldn't use you for them. If you do not believe this, then put it to the test. Set aside a month in which you do not pay for the dates you go on, do not provide for her, do not do special favors for her, or give her any treatment that she does not give you. Treat her as an equal, exactly the way that she treats you. I guarantee you that before the month is up you will find yourself being disrespected, or even emasculated or worse, dehumanized and broken down by her for not giving her what she wants, and then you will be discarded. And this will happen all while treating her with the highest respect and dignity that you thought your dynamic was based upon mutually, but it's not mutual. Women do not respect men, their value for us extends only as far as whatever value that they can extract from us. And that is why in our relations with them they are only kind to us when they are getting something from us, otherwise there is no reason.

7 - The Relativity Of Consent & Legal Double Standards For Crimes By Gender

Only women's consent counts in this culture. Back when I dated I was constantly sexually violated by women as a man, because they didn't see what they were doing as a sexual violation. They didn't even consider me as needing to give consent. They didn't consider me as having sexual rights. Even in the Sex Ed, Kink & BDSM community where people are supposed to be more conscious of consent, I was treated the same way. I was a good Dom would ask for consent for every form of touching until a contract was established. However when I would tell a prospective partner that I wish for my consent to be asked for as well, the common response I would get is "I don't want to have to ask you/I shouldn't have to ask you". And when I ask why, they say "Because I am a woman and you are a man." Why should my consent as man not be asked for? Why should it not count? There is no reason. Because it should. It is wrong that a mans consent would not be asked for when women demand a men asks for theirs first.   But it is just like the Double Standard (hypocrisy) that a man should never hit a woman, not even in his defense if he is being hit by a woman, but it is ok for a woman to hit man. And this is backed by the statistic that most domestic violence is actually female on male, however it doesn't often get reported, and when it does, the woman is never charged, but rather the police will take her side and ask the man to leave. Domestic violence arrests are only made when it is the man striking the woman.   This same standard translates into men constantly getting physically violated by women, because it is not considered assault, since society has not made those boundaries clear for men as it has women.

Even when a man states what he consents to and what his preferences are for being touched, he can actually expect them to be ignored a large portion of the time. I cannot tell you how many times I will tell a girl how I like to be touched, only to have her ignore it, and will also tell a girl not to touch me in a certain way only to have her then do it. I have had so many women grab my ass or even my penis without asking. I even had one instance in which a girl who I was making out with, without any sort of communication about consent, foreplay or seduction, started yanking on my penis, hard! So hard that it hurt! I exclaimed "Ow! Don't do that! That hurts! Why would you go right for my penis anyways we've only just started making out, I'm not even aroused yet haven't you heard of foreplay?" She responded "Sorry", and I told her to do some more foreplay before going there and not to just yank on my penis so hard. But what did she do? Literally not a moment later, she repeated the same exact thing. It was unbelievable. I again called her out on her bad behavior and she said "well I don't know what you want!" Even after I had already told her, a common response I get from women who don't want to do what simple little things I ask for, such as touching me somewhere besides my penis. That's not the worst example though, I also had another girl grab my penis while we were at the beach, and again, did so hard. Hard enough that a couple sea shell fragments mixed in with the sand that had gotten up my shorts cut into the head of my penis, which was incredibly painful. When I exclaimed "ow that hurts", her response was to turn away from me and ignore me. This was technically sexual assault and left my penis injured for a week and in extreme pain.

Unfortunately that was not the only time I have had girls do things to me that could be definitively classified as sexual assault. That is if I bothered to report them, which I do not. And why do you think that is? I have had a drunk girl who I did not know physically assault me in a bar by starting to punch me in the upper arm and shoulder while laughing. And when I reported it to a security guard, his response? He laughed as well. I've had countless women grab my ass while walking by in bars too. When I say "What the fuck, that girl just grabbed my ass!" To whoever is standing next to me, they act like I should have been thankful for the female attention.

I have even had two different women coerce me into having sex with them in a way that fulfilled their fetishes, without any communication or negotiation or consent, and even started dominating me physically without asking. One of these girls started randomly hitting me during sex, and almost ripped my nipple ring off in the process which was very painful. Another started playing out a rape fantasy with me, acting forceful and domineering with an angry look on her face saying "that is my cock you don't even have a choice". These things which could have gone differently and been sexy if they had been pre-negotiated, weren't at all when they happened. They felt like I was being assaulted, because I was. But I can't bother reporting them, because I won't be heard as a man, men simply do not have voices when it comes to consent violations. But imagine if the genders were reversed in these situations and any of the things I had told you about in the last two paragraphs had been done by a man to a woman. That would be an outrage, wouldn't it? Well I as a man still feel violated when I get sexually assaulted, and it still feels bad. And I should have the same sexual rights to things like consent, safety, and speaking out against assault that women have, but I do not.

Paradoxically though consent is more than just a double standard, but female consent itself is even relative. Now of days not only does a mans consent not count, but a woman's consent is starting to not count when he asks for it either. Not in the same way, but rather a very opposite way. For these days you can be a good Dom and ask for consent in every way you need to from a woman, and not only will she not ask yours in return, but she may withdraw her consent after the fact and accuse you of assault/rape for things that were actually perfectly consensual. And in many states a woman's consent is starting to not count if she has had any alcohol to drink, though that is not the same for a man. So two people on a date drinking together who go home and have sex, actually can be seen as rape. The woman's consent didn't count because she was drinking, but it didn't mean anything that the man was drinking. I guess the genders are not equals and the man is always seen as having higher consciousness and accountability than women in the eyes of the law, which seems rather sexist to me.

BDSM contracts are not admissible in court because they are not legally binding. So how can you even trust a woman's consent as a man? Consent doesn't seem to hold the meaning it should with women, but I guess that is the nature of a woman giving her word, they feel that they have the right to change their mind about any agreements or social contracts they have entered into and should be able to do so without consequence. I now am in the middle of a legal battle myself with a girl who had met me on fetlife and contracted me to help her become a porn star and then violated our porn contract, which was legally binding, but which she felt as though she shouldn't have to obey and violated in a number of ways, along with my intellectual property rights, tried to make sales off the record for a larger share of profit, and then when I caught her and told her she had to stop, she didn't, and instead said she wasn't going to work with me anymore and when I hired a lawyer she weaponized the legal system against me and committed perjury on legal documents, defamed my character on public record with false accusations making it seem like she hadn't actually hired me to do porn with her and a contract didn't exist between us, but that it was more like revenge porn, and had me ordered to stop disseminating it. This came from a woman who said to me while signing the contracts that she didn't know why all of the clauses in them were necessary because she would never take me to court or make any false claims against me or anything. And the women who bring men up on false charges do not get in trouble for perjury like they should, because they are women. They are able to bring charges against a man that are damaging to him, even if they do not stick, and have no consequences for their actions what so ever. The justice system is not just, it is gynocentric. Just ask any divorced man.

The same goes for harassment laws. Not only is sexual harassment against men not recognized but a woman can claim sexual harassment from a man when one has not taken place. Women can call the police on a man for harassing her arbitrarily when he was not actually harassing her, or even file a fraudulent restraining order against him when he is not actually harassing her. They often do this in a blatant effort to weaponize the legal system against their exes. And again they will not get into trouble for perjury. But I have had girls who I broke up with who were harassing me or even stalking me and the law would not do anything about it when I called the police. Men have no way of protecting themselves against women, but women can weaponize the law against men.

There is also a growing trend of female sexual predators in the world. I see them in the news more often than I see male sexual predators these days. Most of whom commit their heinous sexual acts against children. And I'm sure its not because they are getting more coverage, but actually less. Because when they do get covered, they are referred to in different ways. They are never called pedophiles when they have sex with a minor as a man is.

They are never said to have "sexually assaulted" or "raped" their victim, but to have "had sex with them". Even though the law clearly states that a minor can not consent to sex with an adult and that such an act is rape. It is never called rape if the predator is a female. And these women get off with far lighter sentences than male sexual offenders.

Unfortunately many female sexual offenders who do not become teachers so that they can fuck their students come to the kink community and start calling themselves Dominatrixes, when they are not even real proper educated Domme's. In fact the vast majority of the Domme's I have met were overtly predatory, and didn't even seem to know the first thing about consent, only about sexual harassment and abusing men. And they felt no need to hide any of this either. They were completely shamelessly predatory, because in this social world it is seen as completely appropriate for a female to act as such (but when a male even begins to act that way, women of course will start calling him out on it). A woman can not only act like a rapist and abuser, but she can even make a living at it! It seems any man hating woman can put on a leather outfit and label herself a Domme without even getting any kind of training in safety. Because no one cares about the safety of men, or the integrity of women. And as for so called "submissive" women in the kink community, almost all of the submissives who have solicited me have also all been predatory and were not actually real submissives, but rather it was just another ploy, a façade like the girls who call themselves "good girls" and are looking for a "gentleman". In the end, they were just looking for a Dominant man to exploit. And again, they didn't have to hide their double standards.

Female predation in our social world is completely socially acceptable, and even somewhat sanctioned by law. While a male teacher who has done anything inappropriate with an underage student will be labelled a rapist, sent to a maximum security prison where he is raped (legally) by other prisoners and when released will be a sex offender with his life ruined, especially professionally, and will never work a good job again. A female teacher who has had sex with an underage male student will not be labelled a rapist but instead will be said to have "had sexual relations" or something putting it lightly to make it sound more appropriate. She will then avoid a harsh sentence, perhaps spending a short time in a lesser prison than the man (if any time is spent in jail at all,) and then afterwards she can use the media attention she garnered which actually made her seem like a sex symbol to men to get a high paying job as a porno model.

That is the gynocentric world we live in.

8 – "Empowerment" "Equality" & Exploitation

Feminists love using the term "Empowerment" and "Empowering" and "Equality" to describe things that they want. But yet these things are reserved for women, and are not amenities afforded to men. Men do not get the same empowerment or equality that women do, so it is not actually equality. And when feminists use the word "Exploitative" they are referring of course to something they do not want that men do to women, or that men experience that puts them at an advantage and women at a disadvantage. Yet there are a plethora of ways in which women exploit men, and feel as though they should be able to, because they find it empowering.

There is no equality for men, in fact men are not even allowed to be empowered in ways that women are not. The standard is this: If something allows women to benefit from men, or for women to benefit and men not to, it is called "empowering". If something allows men to benefit from women or for men to benefit and women not to, it is called "exploitation". Men are simply not granted the same permissions to do these things as women are, they are not allowed to do the very things that women love to do and find so "empowering", and women are allowed to exploit men because it is empowering to them. If there is ever a situation in which a man is at an advantage and a woman at a disadvantage there is political outrage about it and the man is labelled an oppressor, when it is actually the men who are being oppressed. This double standard of women playing the victim and claiming to be so disempowered and exploited is the vehicle they use to make their power grabs with which they oppress us.

A woman marrying a richer man and then divorcing him and taking more money than she came with so that she can be more independent is empowering, a man doing the same thing is seen as exploitative. A woman deciding that she wants to get an abortion due to irresponsible sex, and saying that big daddy government should pay for it, is empowering; but a man who suggests his girlfriend get an abortion when they have a surprise pregnancy, and not offering to pay for it is exploitative. A woman who stops taking her birth control without telling him so that she can get pregnant by a man without his consent and then deciding to be a single mother and keep the child from the man is empowering, but a man who pokes a hole in a condom to get a girl pregnant is exploitative. Additionally, men who are against women being able to take men's money in divorce, against abortion, against prostitution and other careers that objectify women, are also seen as being exploitative towards them. And when it comes to paternity, the double standard is that if a man wants to have power of decision making and be in control of the finances and such, that is him being "patriarchal", but when a woman tries to control him, if he does not do what she wishes or provide for her enough, she will accuse him of not being "paternal" enough. It is a double standard leaving men with no power, no equality, they are being exploited.

There is another example of these double standards that runs far deeper, and that is what happens when men and women are trying to profit off of their sex appeal. For when a woman profits off of her sex appeal by becoming a model, pornographer, or sex worker, it is seen as empowering for her. But if a man uses pornography or prostitutes, he is seen as objectifying women, misogynistic, and creepy. But when happens when a man tries to become a model, pornographer, or sex worker? This is not seen as empowering. And in fact the chances are they will not be able to be successful because the industry hires a small fraction of the men it does women, and so not only are fewer men getting hired, but the standards for them are much higher, and so they are judged far more than women are, and thus are objectified more. The men who do get hired are objectified more than women are ever objectified by men, I know because I am in porn. Women feel it is appropriate to speak publicly about a man's penis size being too small when he shows it, but when it comes to themselves they want body positivity. And feminists obviously have no problem with male models men being objectified and body shamed. Recently during the 2021 olympics, feminists released an article saying that men shouldn't be looking at the female athletes sexually, which is ironic because their physical training makes them some of the top physical specimens in the world, that is what the Olympics is, so of course they would have great sex appeal…yet we are told by feminists to deny this? It is even more ironic because there was also another article released by women recently on male attractiveness, judging men by the most impossibly high physical standards and was the most objectifying thing I have ever read.

Yet feminists have no problem with women objectifying men. And yet while men who make their money off of their looks get objectified more than women, they also get paid a fraction of the amount women do, even if they are doing more work. In fact most women feel as though they shouldn't have to pay for porn, and also wouldn't even buy sex toys from a male sex toy vendor either, and also wouldn't pay for a sensual/sexual massage from a man either and feels that just him getting to touch her in a way that is sexual, or not even sexual but sensual, should be enough compensation for him to want to give her the massage for free. And there's plenty of other products that women will not buy from men either, and professions that men do not do as good as women in. For instance I used to sell women's shoes, but women seemed to want to buy their shoes primarily from other women. The top sales people were women, who had to put in very little effort to make sales, meanwhile I busted my ass trying to make sales and ended up making below the poverty line and going into debt with the company because I wasn't even making enough sales to cover my base pay. But there was no affirmative action for me or the other men like me, no support from my company, or my community, politics, nothing. Yet again, feminists and women in general have no problem with men making less than women in the same exact positions, even though they claim to want there to be equal pay between the sexes. Yet they have had no calls for affirmative action for men in industries such as these that are female dominated and in which women get paid far more.

The same paradigm is seen in both the professional world and the world of dating/relationships/Marriage, and basically anywhere else in society where men and women are interacting, such as the world of politics. Women expect affirmative action and to have to contribute less than men and have men provide for them. In the world of relationships & marriage a successful man can take a poor woman and build her up. But women do not do the same for men. A successful woman would never even give a poor man the time of day as a suitor in dating. In fact not only do women not build men up, but they actually break them down and mine them for resources to extract from them. And what happens to the women that the successful men build up? Well as soon as the women become their equals or begin to outperform them at times, they lose interest. If a woman's husband who she once called her "life partner" goes into a low when the woman is experiencing a high, she will do nothing to help build him back up, but rather she will lose interest in him. In fact women are not even interested in men when they are at an equal level of success. Women's attractiveness is hypergamous and based upon the man being superior to her and having more to offer her than she does him. And when that stops being the case, they lose interest. 80+% of divorces are initiated by women, and often it is due to no fault of the man, she is simply no longer attracted to him because he is no longer that much more her superior. So she leaves him for an even higher status man. This is called hypergamy. The richest man in the world was a self starter who married a less successful woman. The richest woman in the world got her money from marrying and divorcing him. This is not an isolated incident, but is exemplary.

I have been thinking about the supposed equality that is said to exist between men and women a lot lately. My last submissive liked to think of herself as a strong independent woman and kept telling me that we were equals. But yet I was giving 90-95% or more to the relationship and was lucky to get 10% back from her, at maximum. In fact on average it was more like 3% or 5% at best, and sometimes it would actually be 100/0 and I would have to be constantly nagging her about the fact that she wasn't doing anything she said she would and was making me do everything. Eventually I had to realize that this was a pattern, not a series of mistakes. That she just wasn't willing or able to do what I did or give to the relationship or me, what I gave to it and her. So I started wondering how exactly we were equals, if at all.

I did all of the cooking and cleaning, and even when she would try to help I would end up just having to help her do what she was doing, or re-clean things she had "cleaned" afterwards. She wasn't capable of having intellectual conversations with me even about the topics that she brought up, our conversations were always one sided with me doing all of the talking. When it came to communicating about serious relationship oriented things and doing relationship work, again, I was the one doing all of the communicating and relationship work and she would do none. When it came to responsibility, again I was the only one who had any responsibility in the relationship, and she almost never even followed through on any of the things she said she was going to do, it was less than 10% of the time that her word actually meant anything. When we had business projects together, even if it was her idea that would fulfill her dream, I would be doing almost all of the work, like more than 95% of it, and she wouldn't even be able to do the bare minimum, such as printing out and signing legal documents she needed to get to me.

When it came to money, she actually made slightly more money than me, and had fewer expenses, yet she seemed to have more money troubles than me and I ended up paying for everything in the relationship. When it came to support and caregiving, again it was more than 90% me giving and her giving less than 10%, as our conversations were always focused on me giving her emotional support for every little tiny thing that went wrong in her life, when I myself had so many more much larger problems burdening me which she never offered me hardly any moral support with what so ever, and I could hardly depend upon her to help me relax and unwind because I was always having to help her with her minor problems that she would turn into much bigger issues than they were. And last but not least, I am going to be brutally honest with you here, in the bedroom she was a very selfish lover and would get multiple orgasms each time we had sex while I was lucky to have one, and barely ever did anything for my pleasure, I could communicate about my likes and dislikes and would mostly get ignored. Even when it came to thoughtfulness, consideration, affection, romance and love I was the giver and she was the taker.

Across the board she would take and not give, yet would always assert that we were equals. When she would not take care of my needs she would suggest that I date other women as well so that I could find some others who would meet the needs she wasn't, but then would say that since we were equals she would also see another man for every woman I was seeing. Which doesn't seem like equality to me because

I was doing everything she needed of me and she was doing almost nothing I needed of her, not even the things she offered to and said she was going to. Eventually this imbalance, or in other words, inequality, caused the relationship to collapse. Just like a mountain that had been mined for resources until it had been hollowed out so much that it collapsed. So had I by an exploitative woman who took everything she could from me until she had completely depleted me, and then when my usefulness had been diminished and I had no more left to give and demanded that she start making good on her promises, what do you think she did? She left me. She even violated a professional contract that we had between us in multiple ways, violating not only the contract but my very rights, which as I mentioned earlier we are now going to court for. I suppose I should feel lucky that I was not married to her otherwise it could have been so much worse and I could have ended up like 80+% of the married men out there who get half of their assets taken from them by greedy women.

This has me thinking a lot about equality and gender relations because of the fact that this is just one more case in a long pattern. Over the past 18 years of my adult life I have been dating woman after woman with this exact same set of problems. I will have one serious relationship about every year or so that will last about a few months or more before it implodes due to this inequality and thus imbalance. And I will date lots of women in between relationships who don't even claim or try to be equals and so I don't even enter into relationships with them. It just seems that there is never any equality necessary to give the relationship the balance it needs for it to be healthy and sustainable. And it is not because I am dating the same exact types of women. I have dated across many demographics and cultures. Yet it is always the same. The relationships are always a 90/10 split, at best. The women take but do not give. All of the responsibility always falls upon me, and none upon them. I cannot even trust that their word means anything when they give it to me about something they are going to do.

When it used to happen to me I used to think that I had just had a bad experience with a bad girl, and that it was an isolated incident. But this has happened with so many different types of women at this point that I am beginning to think that it is just the way women are. They say they are our equals, but yet their behaviors tell a different story and make it seem like they are actually not. In fact it seems more like they are our exploiters. And this would make sense because of the theory that women are hypergamous. So this means that men like me end up in these situations because women do not want equality. Women are not attracted to their equals. They are attracted to superiority. The relationships they enter are not with men who are their equals but their superiors. And if the man stops being superior over time, which will often happen as she depletes him of his resources and usefulness, she will then leave him, usually without so much as even giving him an explanation (and as we know these days just ghosting someone is very common).

This experience has not just been isolated to dating and relationships either. Whenever I have female friends they are constantly having me help them with things and never offer me anything. And in business it is probably the worst. When I have had female employees, colleagues and affiliates, I can barely count on them to show up for work or meetings. Even when it is an affiliate who I am offering a free promotion of their work for, the women barely ever show up. I was an equal opportunity employer and did my best to work with 50% women but was unable to because I ended up having to invest way too much time head hunting trying to find good female help and being unable to find women who will even show up. However in my entire work history I only ever had one man reschedule at the last minute ever. The men were always dependable. And when I did work with women the work that they did was often of poor quality, and I would end up having to do tons of work on their work to try to bring it up to par, which cost me a lot of time energy and money, and even then I would often not feel good about how it made my company look. I never had this problem with men. And I have heard the same from male friends of mine, that they have to give extra time and energy to help the women they work with do their work, which they can not do on their own. Yet these women get paid the same as men while doing less work and needing men to do portions of their work for them. Women want affirmative action and workplace support of male colleagues and employers because they do not want to be held to the same standards of work load and quality as men are, but yet they want equal pay, because they are exploiting us. Just as they do in relationships with us when getting us to do all of the relationship work, and to contribute more money to the relationship as well (for the shared lifestyle that they do most of the decision making about).

I am going to ask you a serious question now. And I want you to think about it very hard and consider your past experiences and give a thoughtful answer. This is not time for sexism or politics. I want to know: Are women really the equals of men? And if so, what exactly is it that makes them equal? For if we are in fact equals as women say, I cannot see what it is that makes us such. Because at when it comes to:

-Honesty & Integrity

-Communication & Language

-Thoughtfulness

-Responsibility/Dependability

-Effort

-Work & Professional Skill

-Domestic Abilities

-Money Management

-Relationship skills

-Sexual Abilities & Pleasure

I have not seen any equality, or anything even close to it, its been more like exploitation. It's always been 90/10 at best, and that's at very best. At worst it will be even as bad as 100/0 in which the woman basically feels as though her fleeting presence is enough, and has me taking care of her as if she is a small child and I am her father. So if there are areas that women excel at that make them our equals, what are they? Because none of them have made any appearances in my relationships with women yet.

I know what the misandrists are going to say in response to this. They are going to say "you are attracting these women for a reason, because there is something wrong with you." Because that is all I've heard when I try to get relationship advice from this gynocentric community in which the men are always wrong and women are always right. Now I am supposed to believe that being a good man and having a lot to offer a woman is a fault. That I am at fault for getting taken advantage of, exploited and victimized by a bad woman. No, what that is called is victim blaming.

9 – Misandry & Victim Blaming

When a woman mentions having had an abusive ex society says: "You poor girl! It's not your fault! Don't blame yourself! We will do everything we can to help you!" When a man mentions having had an abusive ex, society says: "Man up, take responsibility, you brought this on yourself, stop complaining and move on." When a woman speaks out about abuse against her she is treated by the community as though she is a victim who was targeted. When a man does it he is treated as though he was attracted to bad girls because he has psychological issues and deserves what he got in return.

Men can and do get abused by women. Actually the statistics are in, and it turns out that women are more abusive towards men than men are towards women…and women are even more abusive towards each other too. The most abusive relationships are actually lesbian relationships. Women are simply more abusive people, because society hasn't told them not to be like it does to men. Society teaches boys never to hit girls, but it doesn't teach girls never to hit boys. So women think that they can hit men and that men can't hit back. And they get away with it too. Police are trained to treat the man as the aggressor on any domestic violence call, even if he was the one who called (I know because I've been there plenty of times with my son's mother who was an extremely violent and abusive woman). And if a man tries to report any kind of abuse or assault from a woman he will usually not be taken seriously and the police will not file a report for him. Even if the assault is severe or sexual in nature. Only if a man goes to a hospital with an injury from a woman is he finally seen as a victim in the legitimate legal sense. But men do get abused in relationships constantly by women who are using violence to oppress them. Men even get sexually assaulted by women. And when they report it they are either laughed at (like a security guard who laughed at me when a female assaulted me in a bar), or dismissed coldly. Recently there was a news story of a rich man who was on a date with a woman who seduced him into penetrating her unprotected, and then produced a gun and forced him to ejaculate inside of her so that she could have his offspring and sue him for child support. He went to the police afterwards and they refused to file a report for him and allow him to press charges against her, even though a crime had been committed. He now has to wait to see if she will become pregnant and ruin his future, and if she will be granted child support from the court, which there is little doubt that she will.

Feminists have long asserted that an abused or assaulted woman should never be made to think that it was in any way her fault. That we should not be using language with female victims about how their choices could have lead to it, or how they could have brought it upon themselves. So why is victim blaming ok to do with men? There's enough awareness about not doing it with women that everyone knows how to console a female victim and not make her feel any worse about her possible part of the incident. So why is it the norm to do this very thing with men? Even in groups that are supposed to be support groups for these things I made a post about having an abusive ex, and was victim blamed. Then shamed for having feelings about it. These people act like I was attracted to narcissists and sociopaths and chose them on purpose knowingly. But no one chooses abusers knowing they are going to abuse you, they seduce you into thinking they are going to treat you well. You fall for them for the same reasons you fall for anyone. You think you have a mental and physical connection with them. Sometimes a spiritual one too. They make you think you have found true love, a life partner, someone you could possibly marry. Only to then get lied to and exploited.

When you have an abusive partner who is very good at what they do because they are narcissistic or sociopathic you can tell them when you are feeling disrespected, mistreated, wronged, violated, used, taken advantage of, etc. They will say and do all of the right things to show remorse and make amends and say they will make it up to you and be better. Then when they have restored your confidence its like you said, the cycle of abuse just continues. They are very convincing, and will use gaslighting if necessary. And it will take time for you to have definitive proof that they are in fact lying and manipulating you. Because they have plenty of valid excuses as to why they are not holding up their end of the relationship. By the time you know for sure that they have been doing this all purposely, you will be broken and used up.

Then you come to your local community looking for support, which is what your community is supposed to be there for. And as a man you get told that it is your fault, that you brought this on yourself, and to man up and take responsibility. You are met with lines of "Stop being a whiny little bitch, be a man, you got yourself into this mess, get yourself out." A man cannot even find support in an anti-misandry men's group online and just gets treated with the same misandry and abuse that he gets from women, and there may even be women who have infiltrated the group in order to assert their dominance there and to shut down any male voices they don't like, and even shame them. It is really inappropriate to victim blame anyone of any gender in any situation. You should never tell anyone that abuse was their fault. If I was a woman people wouldn't and would know it is obviously wrong, but yet they do so to a man shamelessly as if they are doing the right thing.

Why is it that everyone knows what victim blaming is when a woman is the victim, but when a man is the victim everyone automatically blames him? And now men aren't even allowed to feel any kind of way about it or they get shamed for that too. We get told that we have issues and are fucked up, when the only thing fucked up is how we are being treated.

It's also interesting that on the other hand I'm being told by other people that it was my fault for not vetting them more, but when I ask them how to vet them more, they won't give me any advice, but rather when I propose ways of vetting them for these types of abusive behaviors, they shoot down my ideas and say that I shouldn't be overprotective. This is the world we live in. A man is damned if he does, damned if he doesn't. People want men vulnerable in this community, we are not supposed to protect ourselves from bad women. We are supposed to take the abuse from them, so that we can then be told that we deserved it. Because that is how feminism wants it. It wants to pretend that women are victims of men so that it can feed women messages of female empowerment and the war on men, justifying female oppression, mistreatment and exploitation of men. Allowing them to get away with victimizing men because they are acting like they are the real victims and men are the real oppressors, when it is actually the other way around. And if any man speaks out about being victimized by a woman, they have pre-loaded messages of victim blaming for that so that they can silence them and maintain their upper hand in the power dynamic.

10 - The Matriarchy We Live In

So why are things able to be so stacked against men? Feminism wants you to believe that we live in a patriarchy in which women are oppressed and need to be more empowered. This is actually nothing more than a manipulation tactic which they use in order to gain more power over men, more rights and freedoms with less responsibilities, and to disempower and take rights away from men. It is very similar to what is called projection in psychology, where you accuse someone of doing something that you yourself are actually the one doing. The truth is that we actually live in a matriarchal sociopolitical, judicial/legal, and economic system. Women are the ruling class and are oppressors of men, and men are becoming more and more like a slave class.

- Women have more rights than men
- Women have less responsibilities than men
- Women have more freedoms than men
- Women are more protected and defended than men
- Women are more supported than men
- Women are held less accountable for their actions than men
- Women are more provided for than men
- Women receive more favor in court, even when they're criminals
- We do not live in a patriarchy, we live in a matriarchy.
- Women are not the oppressed, they are they oppressors.

This is not just rhetoric. In the following several segments I will make the cases and prove how in numerous ways we are living in a matriarchy in which these things are true, just for those of you who are skeptical. Though I'm sure many of you men out there already know what I'm talking about because you've seen it for yourself. But just because I'm a man and I like to speak based upon facts and evidence, I'm going to give you all you need, coming up in the following sections which will be proving that we live in a matriarchy in a large number of ways, each using a number of sources and citations.

Biases In Schooling, Career & Financial Responsibility:

Thanks to affirmative action, women get more scholarships than men and graduate college more than men do, partly due to the fact that women get almost 60% of scholarships and men only get about 40. Women are the majority of teachers/educators, which means women are the majority of those who are influencing the developing minds of the youth and the information they get.   Affirmative action is ushering women into the most cushy jobs in the world (based on their gender not on merit), while men are being left to occupy all of the worst, hardest, most dangerous jobs in the world. Women now earn equal pay as men but yet they do not want to have the same financial responsabilities so they still complain about a false wage gap even though it has been debunked. And they expect men who they date to pay for them, and to be the financial providers in relationships and marriage. Women do not pay taxes, men are the only tax payers and men's tax dollars go to women. Case in point:

College scholarship statistics:
https://whattobecome.com/blog/scholarship-stats/

Women are the majority of teachers:
https://www.brookings.edu/blog/brown-center-chalkboard/2019/03/29/as-more-women-graduate-from-college-the-teaching-profession-becomes-more-female/

Women earn far more college degrees than men:
https://www.aei.org/carpe-diem/stunning-college-degree-gap-women-have-earned-almost-10-million-more-college-degrees-than-men-since-1982/

Women earn more higher degrees, like PhD's, than men:
https://www.aei.org/carpe-diem/women-earned-majority-of-doctoral-degrees-in-2019-for-11th-straight-year-and-outnumber-men-in-grad-school-141-to-100/

Men alone pay taxes, which go to women:
https://femoid.com/its-true-only-men-pay-tax/

Men are 10 times more likely to be killed at work than women:

https://www.forbes.com/sites/chuckdevore/2018/12/19/fatal-employment-men-10-times-more-likely-than-women-to-be-killed-at-work/?sh=7ef06ae452e8

The Sexual Objectification of Men:

Women want everyone to believe that they are sexually objectified and have an impossible standard of beauty, but the opposite is true. In fact most sexual objectification of women and high standards of beauty come from themselves. The truth is that most men do not have very high physical standards for women, as online dating studies show that men are attracted to a large percentage of women, and the aforementioned marriage/divorce statistics show that it is men who want relationships more than women, and women who use men as objects. It is women who have the impossibly high standards, as online dating studies show that women are only physically attracted to an extremely small percentage of the top tier men. And women objectify men more than men do to women, because women treat men as both status objects (in hypergamy) and sex objects as well. Cases in point:

On male sexual objectification:
https://deeraiyenged.wordpress.com/sexual-objectification-research/

The impossible standards of male beauty:

https://goodmenproject.com/featured-content/the-new-and-impossible-standards-of-male-beauty-hesaid/

Women swipe right only a fraction of the time in online dating:

https://www.elle.com/uk/life-and-culture/culture/news/a31293/men-swipe-right-on-tinder-more-than-women-study-confirms/

Tinder Swiping Statistics By Gender in 2020:
https://boostmatches.com/tinder-statistics/#Men_vs_Women_On_Tinder

The attractiveness rating biases on okcupid:
https://www.gwern.net/docs/psychology/okcupid/yourlooksandyourinbox.html

Women's Issues Count And Men's Don't:

Men's issues get marginalized or completely ignored in favor of female issues. Social issues that primarily affect men do not generate awareness or become acknowledged as a serious issue that needs to be solved until it affects women (but once it starts to affect women then it becomes known as a "real issue"). For instance testicular cancer occurs far more than breast cancer, but there is tons of awareness and activism programs for helping women with breast cancer and hardly any for helping men with testicular cancer. And there are plenty of problems that men face such as workplace deaths and suicide that largely go ignored, but when women start to feel so much as depressed, or feel like workplace conditions are unfair, suddenly there is a ton of awareness and activism for those "causes". Even systemic political/legal discrimination against men is either accepted or unnoticed as the entire sociopolitical system we live in is radically biased towards women and it is not seen as an issue. Just think about any social issue that affects women and then ask yourself if it affects men and is still seen as an issue in that case. Now think about any form of sexism against women that feminism has created awareness about and ask yourself if it is also done to men and is seen as sexism when it does. The answers should be clear, but in case they are not, here are the cases in point:

Examples of mens issues that get ignored:
https://listverse.com/2013/06/25/10-examples-of-men39s-issues-the-media-loves-to-ignore/

The systemic discrimination against men:
http://www.jtest28.com/discrimination.html

Systemic Misandry:
https://www.wokefather.com/sexism/misandry-today-
accepting-the-reality-of-baseless-anti-male-hate/

Legal Biases In The Judicial System

The legal system is radically biased towards women. In any case in which the police are called during a dispute between a man and a woman the woman will usually find a way to play the victim and turn the tables on the man and the police will almost always side with the woman and be against the man, even if he was the one calling on her. Police will almost never press charges on a woman on behalf of a man even if she had done something obviously violent and illegal to him. In any court case the courts will usually side with the woman, in family court the rate of this happening is almost 100% of the time. Even when a female is charged with and convicted of a crime she will generally be shown great leniency and not be given the same punishment that men get for the same crime, or may avoid jail time altogether, or get off completely. Even for the worst crimes such as the rape of a child, women will not only usually get off with a slap on the wrist, but will be barely treated as a criminal at all, and the crime will be spoken of as if it wasn't a crime – whenever a female rapes a male child it is not called rape, and she is not called a pedophile, as a man is, it is called "having sex", "sexual relations" or worse yet even a "sexual relationship". Thus women are able to manipulate the legal system in order to get away with criminal acts. Here are some cases to prove these points:

Studies show that judges are gender biased:
https://www.sciencedaily.com/releases/2018/04/1804191415
41.htm

Skeptics analyze biases in the judicial system:
https://skeptics.stackexchange.com/questions/14373/is-the-judicial-system-biased-against-men

Men are more likely to be sentenced to prison than women:
https://goodmenproject.com/ethics-values/sentencing-gap-men-likely-go-prison-mrzs/

Study shows men get longer prison sentences than women for same crime:
https://www.huffpost.com/entry/men-women-prison-sentence-length-gender-gap_n_1874742

Some of the instances in which female teachers raped their young boy students and it was not even called rape:

https://klyker.com/female-teachers-caught-sleeping-with-students-41-photos/

https://www.dispatch.com/news/20190603/more-female-teachers-caught-having-sex-with-students-experts-say

https://heavy.com/news/2018/06/teacher-sex-offender-allegations-female-photos/

https://www.cbsnews.com/pictures/notorious-teacher-sex-scandals/4/

https://abcnews.go.com/US/brittni-colleps-texas-teacher-group-sex-students-shes/story?id=17338821

Marriage Is An Institution of Financial Exploitation Of Men For Female Benefit:

It is socially acceptable for women to use men for their money and resources. They are hypergamous – this is the scientific term that means that they primarily mate with and marry men who are higher status and richer or have more assets/resources than them so that they can elevate their own status and wealth/resourcefulness, and then they continue to repeat this with other men, raising their status and wealth each time. No fault divorce law has facilitated womens ability to treat marriage and divorce as a financial transaction in which they are completely legally able to marry and divorce a man without any other reason other than to take half of his money. More than 50-60% of marraiges end in divorce, 70-80% of divorces are initiated by women, 85 to 90% of custody awards go to the women. Women using marriage and divorce as a financial scam to exploit a man for his resources is not only legal but socially acceptable, as women speak openly about primarily wanting a man for his money, and will tell each other openly to find a man who they can use for his money, women even teach their daughters to do this. All of the richest women in the world have made their money by either doing this, or inheriting it from their fathers.

Facts on the divorce biases:

https://www.askmen.com/daily/austin_60/92b_fashion_style.html

The best way for women get rich is to get married and
divorced:

https://www.dailymail.co.uk/news/article-2312860/How-ex-
wives-super-wealthy-way-rich-list-divorce.html

Only 2 out of the 100 richest women made their own money,
the rest inherited it from men:

https://www.dailymail.co.uk/news/article-2632136/Britains-
1-000-richest-people-DOUBLED-wealth-crash-Mega-
wealthy-combined-wealth-519-billion.html

Legal Biases in Parenting and Family Court

Men have no reproductive rights, women have all the reproductive rights. It is completely legal for a woman to sexually assault a man and steal his sperm. Women can sue a man for child support for just about any reason, even if they are not married and he is not even the father. Women will sue a man for child support who is not the father instead of suing the father for child support, simply because the real father is harder to find or makes less money than their boyfriend.   And the worst part is that paternity fraud is completely legal. This is technically gender discrimination, which should be a civil rights violation, but since it is done by the government it is not seen as one.

Women know all of this and thus they are able to completely weaponized the family court system against men. Often they will even make false allegations of the man being abusive in order to get their way, and will be successful in it because abuse does not have to be proven in order to get a restraining order and once a restraining order is in place it can be used against the man in court. Women will often even weaponized and use a mans children against him in order to manipulate or hurt him using psychological warfare. They do this for the same reasons they get divorces (and often get married) – to take money from men. Women can take children away from a good father for any reason, even when it is obviously wrong for them to do so. Women are awarded custody of children almost 100% of the time, even if they are abusive to them and the man is not.   And in rare cases when the man is awarded custody of a child, they are less likely to get child support from the mother, even if they are awarded child support in court, mothers more often fail to pay it than fathers do. And fathers are often jailed for non-payment, even though it is unconstitutional to imprison someone for not being able to pay their debts.   Cases in point:

Woman forces man to ejaculate inside of her at gunpoint, police refuse to press charges:

https://www.globalnea.com/woman-forced-dogecoin-millionaire-to-ejaculate-inside-her-at-gunpoint/?fbclid=IwAR1OALu6f519WahROlzhKjlr_1zguJZXInabR3J6anlv7ZDn45r1wP4Zwcg

Man is forced to pay child support after an adult woman commits statutory rape against him when he was just a 14 year old boy:
https://www.korolandvelen.com/blog/2014/september/forced-to-pay-child-support-for-child-he-never-k/

Hermesmann v Seyer, the legal case which set the precedent that a woman can sue a man for child support even if conception occurred due to the female raping the male:

https://en.wikipedia.org/wiki/Hermesmann_v._Seyer

The gender bias/discrimination in family court:
https://www.cor-law.com/blog/women-get-child-custody-90-percent-cases-isnt-gender-discrimination/

Facts on child support biases:
https://dadsdivorce.com/articles/dads-represent-85-of-child-support-providers-pay-more-than-female-payers/

Man forced to pay child support to his girlfriend (not wife) for a child that is not his:
https://www.foxnews.com/us/texas-man-ordered-to-pay-65g-in-child-support-for-kid-who-isnt-his

The laws about paternity, which are extremely biased towards women and against men:

https://www.hg.org/legal-articles/can-i-be-required-to-pay-child-support-if-the-child-isn-t-mine-46953

Women using children as weapons against fathers:
https://www.dailymail.co.uk/femail/article-1314131/The-cruelty-women-use-children-weapons-divorce.html

Malicious Mother Syndrome:

http://www.parentalalienation.com.au/node/11

Abusive mother gets custody, father gets thrown in jail for trying to protect son:
https://www.ebaumsworld.com/videos/heartbreaking-video-of-the-moment-an-alleged-abusive-mother-gets-custody-of-her-son/85790804/

Women Are Violent Abusers and Oppressors Of Men:

What if I told you that domestic violence wasn't so much a problem that affects women, as it is men. What if I told you that most domestic violence wasn't actually perpetrated by men against women, but by women against men, or other women? You wouldn't believe me of course, because of the great degree of propaganda that feminists have churned out about domestic violence, painting women as the perpetual victims of it and men as the toxic predatory aggressors who must be jailed for their heinous crimes. But what if I told you that in many if not most cases in which the man has actually gotten violent with the woman, that she actually was violent with him first and he was either defending himself or engaging in a fight with a woman (who is supposed to be his equal in the eyes of feminism), who has chosen to start a physical fight with him.

What if I told you that what happens even more than that is a woman getting physically abusive and violent with a man and him having no ability to defend himself physically or legally. That when men call the police on a female aggressor they often fail to file a report and won't even allow him to press charges, or when they do, they charges end up getting dismissed in court. Or that worst yet, oftentimes when men call the police on a girlfriend who is behaving abusively, that she often will manipulate them into believing that he was the abusor and getting him kicked out of his own house or even arrested without evidence. What if I told you that this whole time that feminists wanted you to believe that women are innocent victems and men are inherently abusive, that it was actually the other way around, and that we have all been fooled by a set of double standards that we have been brainwashed into believing so that women can get away with abusing men. And what if I told you that actually the most domestic violence occurs in lesbian relationships, because women are really more inherently abusive people than men are. Is this starting to sound believable yet? Is it starting to ring any bells of past experiences you have had with women, or people you know have had?

Lets get to the bottom of this and see what the facts really are. Below are a list of several links from all of the most major and credible news outlets detailing credible evidence based reports how women have actually fooled us about this domestic violence issue so that they can get away with being the abusors. Get the facts, and lets stop letting women manipulate and abuse us and get away with it. Women actually do perpetrate domestic violence more than men do. They know they can get away with it because most men will not defend themselves because they have been taught since they were children to never hit a girl, and there has been enough other propaganda making women out to be innocent victims and men as toxic aggressive animals. And again, if they call the police the police will take the woman's side because that is what police are trained to do. In fact it is so socially acceptable for a woman to beat a man that she can do it in public and no one will care, actually some people find it funny. And there are no social programs or resources or shelters for men who are victims of domestic violence like there are in abundance for female victims, in spite of the fact that female on male domestic violence occurs more. So it turns out, all along, we have been seeing the abusors as the victims, and supporting the wrong people.

It is time we stood up to women, and started supporting the real victims, which is men. Because there are so few social programs out there to help men who are victims of domestic violence, as they often are. While there are over 2,000 shelters for female victims of domestic violence in the USA, which are state run and funded by taxpayer dollars, of which men are paying at least half, almost none of them help men, and there is only one that exclusively does. Men like me who are in DV situations and need to get out of the home even if it means becoming homeless, are sent by the state to mens shelters that double as halfway houses for criminals just getting out of jail where we can experience further assault, even sexual assault, as I did. This is because it is widely believed even by the legal system that men cannot be victims of abuse, or anything but abusors when it comes to domestic violence. And the police are against men as well, if a man calls the police on a woman who is assaulting him, if she even so much as breaks a nail doing so, he will be the one arrested for assault. Men have no human right to defend themselves against female abuse, men have no social support when they are victims. The programs and messages on Domestic Violence all are actually misandristic and anti-male.

https://thenewamerican.com/women-more-likely-to-commit-domestic-violence-studies-show/

https://time.com/2921491/hope-solo-women-violence/

https://news.ufl.edu/archive/2006/07/women-more-likely-to-be-perpetrators-of-abuse-as-well-as-victims.html

https://www.independent.co.uk/news/uk/home-news/women-are-more-violent-says-study-622388.html

https://www.mintpressnews.com/woman-aggressor-unspoken-truth-domestic-violence/196746/

https://www.researchgate.net/publication/222426549_Wome
n_Who_Perpetrate_Intimate_Partner_Violence_A_Review_o
f_the_Literature_With_Recommendations_for_Treatment

https://www.sciencedirect.com/science/article/abs/pii/S13591
78906000474

http://www.newscastmedia.com/domestic-violence.htm

http://liberalamerica.org/2014/05/29/watch-what-happens-
when-a-woman-abuses-a-man-in-public-video/

DOMESTIC VIOLENCE: THE TWELVE THINGS
YOU AREN'T SUPPOSE TO KNOW A Book
(Adventure Press, 2208 Cabo Bahia, Chula Vista, CA
91914., year 2003) – By **James, Thomas, Esq.** In this
book, the author conducts a meticulous and thorough
examination of the research on domestic violence,
coming to the unsettling conclusion that virtually
everything we think we know about domestic abuse is
wrong. Exposing evidence of a deliberate governmental
campaign to distort the truth and proliferate lies,
attorney Tom James, who served as co-counsel with
John R. Graham in a lawsuit to declare battered
women's laws unconstitutional, explains why honesty
and candor are our only real hope for bringing an end to
this enormous social problem.

Women Are More Aggressive, Violent & Tyrannical Leaders:

Have you ever heard feminists say that if the world was run by women it would be more peaceful and there would be no war? Like with domestic violence as described in the last section, this is just manipulative propaganda. And the truth is the opposite way around. You see, female violence isn't just confined to domestic situations. But for the same reasons, women are more violent in general (they can get away with it because they are seen as less violent by nature). This means that women in general are able to behave more aggressively and violently towards men in order to oppress them. And women in power are more aggressive than their male counterparts, and female rulers wage war more frequently than male leaders do. For just as how society gives women permission to be abusers of men, they also allow for women to be tyrannical leaders.   Cases in point:

Female rulers are more likely to wage war:
https://www.eviemagazine.com/post/history-says-that-female-leaders-are-more-likely-to-wage-war-than-men?fbclid=IwAR30JxU1KmHFcTDgZS-a6rXnMCsc9RaRdwkgf07sfaUnXANXs_6dOAb93uk

In the past 500 years queens have waged war more than kings:
https://www.dailymail.co.uk/sciencetech/article-4454964/Female-rulers-27-likely-wage-WAR-males.html

Women Mistreat And Manipulate Men:

Women tend to see men as resources to be taken advantage of and exploited. Due to their hypergamous nature they do not see or treat men with humanity, but see them as objects to be used, and abused if he resists, and then discarded when their usefulness has run out. It is common and socially acceptable for women to manipulate, use, control and psychologically abuse men for their own gain. And they get away with it due to feminism, social gender biases, and their ability to use dark psychological tactics such as reverse psychology and playing the victim when they are actually the victimizer, the oppressed when they are the oppressor, and other such role reversals to keep the tables turned on the man they are exploiting. Here are some of the common ways they do these things:

The Manipulated Man Synopsis & Audiobook:

https://en.wikipedia.org/wiki/The_Manipulated_Man

https://www.youtube.com/watch?v=v2687RHEhGI

https://www.youtube.com/watch?v=qwShlUZuqtw

How Women Control Men In Relationships:
https://thepowermoves.com/female-relationship-control/

How women emotionally abuse men:

https://www.intellectualtakeout.org/blog/women-who-emotionally-abuse-men/

Anti Male Pro Female Gender Bias & Double Standard Explained (Gamma Bias):

Gamma bias is a type of double standard that is formed from the combination of alpha bias and beta bias. Alpha bias is when the differences between the genders are maximized. Beta bias is when the differences between the genders are minimized. Gamma bias is when you do both at different times in order to tip the scales of perception in one direction. In other words, a double standard.

When men are responsible for doing good, for instance how most firemen, are men, the gender differences are minimized, feminism focuses on the fact that there are any female firemen at all, and says that both men and women are responsible for saving people from fires, so they shouldn't even be called fire men, but fire people.

However when men are responsible for doing something bad, for instance the fact that terrorists are almost all male, then feminism focuses on that difference, saying "See there are no female terrorists, only men are terrorists, what does that tell you about men?"

Similarly when a woman invents something feminists will put her on a pedestal for doing it. But they will ignore the fact that it has previously already been invented by men. And when a woman does something bad feminism will not make it about gender difference, but say that it is part of a bigger social issue that effects both genders, or they may actually make it about how women have been oppressed by the patriarchy and that they aren't given enough social support.

You have probably heard feminists and women saying that there are no difference between the genders. They are saying this when they are trying to say that women can do anything that men can do. Which they say when women are aspiring to be like men. So when they noticed that there still aren't enough women in STEM fields, they say "there's no difference in the genders so there shouldn't be less women in the STEM fields". However, anytime a woman actually accomplishes something they will make it seem like women are better than men. So when a woman has become a successful business owner they will make it seem like she did so because she is so much better than men are, in spite of the fact that what she is doing has been done by men infinitely before, and more successfully as well.

Gamma bias is basically a distortion in the perception of gender and the ways in which the genders differ, and the ways in which they are equal. It attempts to make them seem equal where they aren't, and make them seem different where they aren't, both in ways which make women seem favorable and make men seem unfavorable.

In an argument or debate when someone does this it is called moving the goal posts. This occurs when they are making their candidate/party seem better by making its goal posts closer, and making the other seem worse by making its goal posts seem further. They will say "see look at all the wins my guy is making", while they will say "these other guys haven't accomplished anything yet", by moving their goal posts, even though the candidates may have both done about equal in their time campaigning.

So now that you understand what gamma bias is and how it actually makes society biased against men and for women, here is a video that will go over the 4 definitive ways in which gamma bias occurs.

https://www.youtube.com/watch?v=LHYRYKCIDxk

"Toxic Masculinity":

Feminism & the Gynocentric Matriarchy have created and promoted the concept of "Toxic Masculinity", which basically states that masculinity as we know it traditionally is inherently toxic and harmful (as opposed to femininity which isn't of course. Yet there is no real definition for "toxic masculinity", what women mean when they say this is "men are toxic", or "masculinity is inherently toxic", which are erroneous ideas.

Toxic behavior does not occur simply because of ones gender. There are well behaved men, called gentlemen, just as there are well behaved women called ladies. However there are also badly behaved men, and women too. In fact if we were to compare many common male and female behaviors, I think us men can agree that women are far more toxic. They create more drama. They escalate things into arguments more quickly. They are quicker to get physical. Quicker to call the police even though they are the instigator/aggressor. And women will throw anyone under the bus that gets in their way. If feminists want to talk about toxic masculinity, in order for there to be equality, we need to talk about toxic femininity. How women will manipulate others for their personal gain. How they will use their sexuality and seduction to get what they want from men, and then use family courts as a legal weapon to take him for all he's got. How about all the female abusors and male victims with no legal recourse if she calls the police on him with another false accusation because of a fight that she started and he tried to end. How about all the lies and betrayal and cattiness with other females? How about all the narcissism and sociopathy?

Do women have any sort of moral code of ethics that they live by? No, in fact it is men who are known for that.

Women are known for their toxic behaviors. Men know that any time you have a woman in your ear she will be poison dripping you constantly over time to try to wear you down and dominate you so she can take control of you and be able to bend you to her will. And women know how they are socially, that they can't really trust any of their female friends, that female social circles are webs of lies and deceit. Let's face it, women are toxic. And the whole toxic masculinity campaign was just a projection, just like male privilege when women are actually the privileged ones.

Women take so many more liberties with bad behaviors than men do because they know they can get away with it when the cops are called. So next time you hear anyone talk about toxic masculinity, call them out on it and remind them that women are more toxic than men. And what the term toxic masculinity really is is just a misandristic slur against men, and we shouldn't have to stand for that kind of language. If feminists say that they don't want men to say sexist things against them then they shouldn't be so hypocritical as to turn around and do it to us. But hypocritical projectsions are what they do best, so anytime you catch them doing it, call them out for it! Because women are actually the more toxic and harmful of the 2 genders! (Yes, of course there are only 2).

And so in order to have a gender equal discussion about toxicity in behavior, and since we've already discussed toxic masculinity, lets talk next about the idea of Toxic Femininity, and unpack everything that there is in that concept.

"Toxic Femininity"

Female behavior is traditionally toxic and harmful in even
more ways than mens. They are so manipulative that they'll
have you believe that the only ways women can be "toxic" is
if they are holding themselves back, or other women back, by
having a patriarchal attitude that causes them to perpetuate
mysoginistic ideals. But toxic femininity is not when women
act misogynistic towards other women and try to get them to
"be more feminine" or more traditional or something.
Somehow feminists have even found ways to use this term
for their own agenda. But female nature does have its own
negative toxic tendencies. So here I will expose the truth
about toxic femininity and womens actual toxic traits. Which
are numerous:

-Superficiality

-Narcissism & Entitlement & other egomaniacal behavior

-Condescension and belittling of others

-Drama & Argumentativeness

-Clicks & Rivalries

-Scheming

-Gossipping and spreading negative rumors about others to
destroy their reputation

-Violation of boundaries, invasion of others privacy & even
male spaces

-Sociopathic social climbing, doing things such as
befriending people and using them for help and then
discarding them or even throwing them under the bus to get
ahead

-Lying

-Manipulation

-Cheating

-Breaking promises and commitments, flaking on obligations, no show appointments and cancellations without any good reason, etc (when she had given these people reason to depend upon her being there, and her not doing so has a negative impact upon them and their schedule, business, or whatever it may be)

-Hypocrisy and double standards (always being right and always making others out to be wrong, even when she has wronged them)

-Rampant consumerism, hoarding and deep financial debt (for which she will not want to be held responsible, and which leads her to the next one)

-Using and exploiting others for her benefit, namely men in gold digging hypergamy

-Unhealthy romantic relationships, codependence, controlling and coercive behavior

-Seduction and using sexuality for manipulative purposes

-False accusations

-Shaming language

-Harassment and verbal abuse (such as swearing, name calling, trying to break down someones sense of identity (something that is a very psychopathic thing to do))

-Psychological warfare

-Raising voice and not allowing others to speak, even screaming

-Sexual objectification of herself, and other men and women

-Misandry

-Political Correctness Policing (wokeness & such) and campaigning against others for disagreeing and using free speech to voice their opinions

-Refusal of responsibility, blame shifting

-Victim blaming men for female abuses against them

-Physical violence, especially in the female style of slapping, scratching, etc

-Sexual extremism (frigidity and asexuality, promiscuity & hyper sexuality & sex addiction, and sexual deviance and fetishism)

-Spreading STD's (Women catch STD's more easily than men due to the large amount of surface area in the vagina for them to do so, they then go on to use condoms less than men because they don't like to have to buy things for sex or plan and prepare for it, or talk about having safe sex, due to all of their sexual issues, and then they have sex with more men on average than men do with women and are generally all around more promiscuous and sexually reckless, hence them using abortion as a form of contraception which is also a highly toxic trait. I mean choosing to murder your own baby instead of just using a condom? That should tell you how psychopathic these bitches are. And another thing that will show you how psychopathic they are is that some women who get an STD decide to take revenge upon all men and try to spread it on purpose, as documented in the book "why women have sex", so beware of seductive women, their sexuality may be toxic…quite literally!

-The emasculation and dehumanization of men, it doesn't get more toxic than that.

Man Hating & Anti-Male Attitudes:

Whereas women used to be the ones who suffered from sexism and limitations being placed upon their sexual rights and freedoms, as well as other rights and freedoms, women now have all the sexual freedom they could possibly want or need, but it is men who are now sexually shamed and oppressed by womens anti-male sexism. This is because due to feminism we live in a society in which there is now a war on men and masculinity. Women have convinced the world that masculinity is inherently toxic and that men are not only inherently bad but predatory and should all be treated like rapists, because we live in a "rape culture".

Women want you to believe that while men are all inherently either bad or potentially bad, femininity is inherently good…when in actuality it is really the more toxic and tyrannical of the two, as we have seen in the previous chapters. Women have normalized misandry (female on male sexism) and man hating and made it completely socially acceptable to spout sexist hate speech towards men and masculinity. Yet it is not considered sexism or hate speech, in fact feminists state that there is no such thing as misandry and that it is just not possible and that the only way sexism can exist is when it is male on female – that is how deep the sociopolitical manipulation and war on men goes, to the point where they completely deny and invalidate men's experiences of sexist oppression and attacks on our gender, and even go as far as to attempt to brainwash us into thinking that misandry isn't even a real thing! When if it wasn't, there wouldn't be a fucking word for it, would there be?! And conversely they have also made it so that saying anything critical about a female could be called sexism and hate speech and any man doing so will face great consequences.

This war on men and all the misandry and hatred is incredibly destructive to men, and needs to stop. Let me tell you something, In trying to find articles giving examples of misandry for some of the previous chapters, even searching through multiple pages on 2 different search engines I was mostly only able to find articles from feminists denying that it is even a thing, minimizing it as an issue, defending women's right to do it, or just doing it (articles saying things such as "kill all men"), and the fact that this is what comes up on search engines when searching for "examples of misandry" should illustrate the problem (and if you don't believe this problem exists, I urge you to go ahead and search that phrase and see for yourself). But here is the one single article I found on what it is and how it can occur which you can read in the link below.

You may be wondering, how can we know misandry for sure when these feminists are gaslighting us into thinking it isn't even a real thing? Well a really easy way to be able to detect it is to simply consider if the genders were reversed in this situation, would this be called misogyny? Because if the answer is yes, but the genders in the current situation are a woman doing it to a man, guess what, it's still sexism! Yes that's right! So you have just confirmed that what you are dealing with is in fact misandry. And women are constantly saying and doing things to men that they know they would call sexism if the genders were reversed. And since women do not have to deal with sexism, neither should us men. Especially if we are not treating them sexistly, we certainly do not deserve it in return, we deserve to be treated as equals and the same way that we treat them. But obviously feminism missed the golden rule of treat people hwo you wish to be treated…and how you tell them they have to treat you. So no we do not have to put up with that kind of sexist hypocrisy and double standards. The only reason we have been, is because we have been living in a gynocentric matriarchy and have been brainwashed into thinking that we don't have much of a choice. But it is time for us to rebel and start to stand up for ourselves against the systemic misandry of our society. So that concludes my series proving the case that we live in the matriarchy, and the final source I have to cite for you to finish making this case is on the topic of misandry, found on the psychology wiki website, which really breaks down the concept of misandry and is quite a thorough deep dive into different aspects of it, so check that out below.

https://psychology.wikia.org/wiki/Misandry

11 – Civil Rights & Discrimination

The big problem with all of the types of misandry that I have listed is that it is happening not just because it is commonly accepted, but it is commonly accepted because it is not consider civil rights violations, (which aren't easy to prove and legislate for). But yet there are some very basic civil rights that women have that men do not, and ought to. So lets talk about the forms of real illegal civil rights discrimination against men, and then what men's rights are needed.

Discrimination Against Men:

You have probably heard a lot about the discrimination
that women face, but did you know that men face
discrimination as well? It's true! Yet you never hear about it
for some reason. So here are the 5 biggest ways that men
face discrimination today:

1.) Women are exponentially more likely to get
callbacks for job applications. I noticed that once
feminism entered its 4th wave, anytime I would need
extra work and would send out resumes I would get
barely any callbacks whereas I used to get many.
Apparently I am not the only man who has
experienced this problem. Recently I saw a reddit
post which I am linking below where a man sent out
100 resumes as a man, and a woman. They were the
same except gender. The female resume got 650%
more callbacks.
2.) Family Court is extremely discriminatory towards
fathers and biased towards mothers, they almost
always take the children away and give them to the
mother, and award her child support which can never
be reduced even when he loses income.
3.) The police are extremely discriminatory towards men
and biased towards women and always take the
womans side against the man even when he is the one
who called about her harming him.
4.) In sexual assault, any woman can bring any man up
on charges and ruin his life. However if a man is
sexually assaulted by a woman he has no legal
recourse and won't get taken seriously if he attempts
to press charges. Female sexual assault is actually
legal in many places – it is not considered a crime

because it is not considered possible for a woman to sexually assault a man. But when it comes to men being accused by women, the women are always believed unless the man brings definitive proof that it was consensual. In these cases the man is guilty until proven innocent (a violation of his constitutional rights). Even if he proves his innocence then he has still been put through the ringer and had serious damage done to his reputation and life.

5.) Men are perceived and treated as abusers much more than women are, even when the same behaviors are compared. Studies have shown that when people are surveyed about behaviors, the same behaviors in men and women are seen as abusive by men but not by women. I've linked this study below. And there have been numerous social experiments done that show that when a man and woman are arguing aggressively in public, that people will come to the womans aid when the man is just a little bit verbally aggressive, but the woman can become extremely physically aggressive and the man will be laughed at for it.

Sources:

Job Application Discrimination

https://www.reddit.com/r/TrueOffMyChest/comments/jvuzgu/i_sent_100_applications_as_a_man_and_a_woman_its/

Male Vs. Female Behaviors Being Seen As Abusive

https://www.researchgate.net/publication/8006596_Psychologists'_Judgments_of_Psychologically_Aggressive_Actions_When_Perpetrated_by_a_Husband_Versus_a_Wife

Mens Rights (Needed):

I'm sure you've spent your life hearing an aweful lot about womens rights, and very little, if anything at all, about mens rights. Most people are surprised by the topic of mens rights, because they think that men have all the rights they could possibly need and do not think that they could possibly need anymore, that they have more than enough rights, far more than women do. But that is simply not true at all. Women actually do have more rights than men, and men are lacking in this department. This may come as a surprise to you, or maybe not. But at some point in life a man is faced with situations in which his lack of rights and the fact that women's rights trump his becomes painfully apparent. And so we need to outline the rights that men need in this society and create awareness about these issues.

First lets outline the rights that women have that men do not:

1. Women have the right to genital integrity and not have genitals mutilated at birth.
2. Women can vote without having to sign up for the draft and do not have to fight in wars without signing up of their own accord.
3. Women have the right to choose parenthood by any means necessary.
4. Women have the right to be assumed caregivers for children and be automatically awarded custody by family court.
5. Women have the right to call unwanted sexual contact assault and press charges.

6. Women have the right to lower jail sentences for the same crime.
7. Women have the right to not be assumed sexual predators.
8. Women have the right to government departments that solely serve their interests.
9. They also have the luxury of "women only" events that men cannot even dream of. (They even took the boy scouts away from us).
10. Women have the right to government-enforced gender quotas in businesses.
11. Women have the right to exclusive tax benefits for being a business owner.
12. Women have the right to domestic violence shelters
13. Women have the right to not be assumed the primary aggressor in a domestic depute.

So what rights do men need that they do not have? Here are the basics.

1.) Equal reproductive rights and protection from paternity fraud (which should be treated like other forms of fraud) and unjust child support payments
2.) The abolition of no fault divorce
3.) Equality for fathers in family court when it comes to child custody and child support
4.) Unbiased Equality in the legal system and law (namely in cases involving a man vs a woman), and equal sentencing for women.
5.) The right to press charges against women for harassment & assault
6.) The right to self defense against female attackers

7.) The right to press charges against women for making
false accusations
8.) Equal job hiring rights and business rights, & the
Abolition of Affirmative Action for women as well
as gender quotas for businesses
9.) Equal Scholarships at Universities
10.) The right to not have genitals mutilated by
circumcision as a child
11.) The right to equal government and social support
systems such as domestic violence victim support
12.) The right to male only spaces

Until men get these civil rights they will be treated like second class citizens by women and society at large. And we need to show feminists and everyone else that we know what rights we do not have and what it is that we need. We need to keep talking about this stuff and creating awareness abou tit and pushing for it until we live in a just system that legally treats men and women as equals, just like it is supposed to. So make sure you do your part and share this information, and remember these rights and assert the need for them the next time it comes up in conversation and you hear some feminist BS about womens rights and how men have more than they do. Remember that that is just a ploy to trick us into letting them get more, and so far they are getting away with it. Women have gone through every bit of legislation that favored men and made it so that they were equals. But then left the parts of legislation that favored women. So it is time that we tip the scales into balance. Women treat men like they do not deserve the same human rights that they do because they do not see us with humanity. But we are human, and we deserve the same human rights. Not having them is sexism, it is discrimination on the basis of gender, which in our case is called misandry, and it goes against the civil rights act. We need to stand up and speak up for our rights and fight for them, just like feminism has. Men are human beings, we are not slaves, and we will not lay down for women.

Speaking of laying down for women, what about sexual rights? We need to extrapolate upon them, because those are more skewed than anything. Just look at the differences between men's and women's reproductive rights:

Mens Reproductive Rights Before Sex:

1.) Abstain from sex
2.) Pull out, cum elsewhere
3.) Condom
4.) Vasectomy

Mens Reproductive Rights After Sex:

NONE! - Not even once sex has begun!

Womens Reproductive Rights Before Sex:

1.) Abstain from sex
2.) Female condom (or male condom)
3.) Fertility Awareness Method
4.) Birth Control Pill
5.) Diaphragm
6.) Cervical Cap
7.) Sponge
8.) Patch
9.) Nuvaring
10.)Spermacide
11.)Hormone Shots
12.)Hormone Implant
13.)IUD

14.)Tubal Ligation
15.)Female Vasectomy

Women's Reproductive Rights After Sex:

1. To choose whether to allow the man to ejaculate
    inside of her vagina or elsewhere.
2. To try to get herself pregnant, even without the mans
    consent by any means necessary, including forcing
    him to cum inside of her by holding him inside of her
    and not letting go until he does, taking herself off of
    birth control without his knowledge, poking a hole in
    the condom, getting the condom out of the garbage
    and using his semen, or even holding him and gun
    point and forcing him to cum inside of her.
3. Morning After Pill
4. To get an abortion (depending on location) and not
    have to pay for it usually either
5. To give up the child for adoption with or without the
    mans consent
6. To keep the baby and sue the man for child support
7. To commit paternity fraud in order to get a richer
    man than the real father to pay more for child support
    than the real father could, which is actually not
    legally seen as a form of fraud but is totally legal in
    most places

Your seed is sacred, don't give it away. However,
Feminism, paired with lack of rights to their own offspring,
has caused men to stop mating and reproducing with women.
Feminists say the future is female. But with no mating,
reproductive power will lie solely with men. You see, test

tube babies need only male ingredients. & If women want to reproduce, they still need the male ingredients.

12 – Conclusion:
In Defense Of Masculinity

I wrote all of this as a man who is actually considered above average in most departments, and who has actually had a lot of success with women in my 24 years of being sexually active. I've had sex with almost a hundred women, casually dated and had some form of connection with hundreds more. Been in what seemed like love several times and had a few serious long term relationships. I even had a child with a woman who was my best friend and longest relationship when I was younger. And I've been involved in Kink/BDSM for almost a decade now and had a lot of epic experiences with it. And yet even with all of that success and all of the good things I've experienced in dating, there's been so much bad to go along with it that it almost negates the good. All of the feeling used and exploited. Being abused both mentally and physically and having no support for the trauma it causes because I am a man. Being sexually assaulted and having it not even be considered sexual assault. All of the heart break and devastation from being broken up with (and women are very sociopathic when breaking up with a man). And even some legal battles, which are a very difficult thing to have to go through.

After writing all of this, it has me thinking, wow, and this is me complaining about all of this as a man who has been successful with women and had so many good experiences too. I can't even imagine just how bad it would be for a man who is below average and is considered unsuccessful with women and has it worse than me. Someone who has to deal with mainly bad experiences and not so many good ones, experiences which are even worse than mine. A man who might have even married a woman and was good to her and then gotten cheated on and divorced for no reason and had half of his assets and his kids taken away from him and left not only heart broken and unable to see his kids except every other weekend, but also financially devastated. As this is the most common end result for marriage today. And that's not even the worst you could expect from dating. And that's not even as bad as it gets. Some men these days even find themselves brought up on false rape charges because they sleep with a girl who gives her consent before sex but then later regrets it because her boyfriend found out she cheated on him and she has to lie and say she was raped, and the mans life gets ruined, even if he doesn't end up getting convicted, but if he does, he then has to go to jail and get raped himself, and then when he gets out he has to live his life as a sex offender. And all because an evil manipulative sociopathic narcissist needed to cover up her lying and cheating, she will ruin an innocent mans life in the worst way possible.

These are just a couple examples of women's common destructive tendencies towards men. Not to mention all the gold diggers out there using men like ATM machines under the premise of love. Or all of the female on male domestic violence. The list of ways that women use and abuse men goes on and on. And again, this is because we live in a misandristic paradigm that is sexist towards men, and beyond just prejudice or discrimination, we are downright oppressed and abused. Why do you think that we are partially castrated at birth, which is an obvious human rights violation that is accepted (while female genital mutilation is spoken out against) simply because it is profitable to the establishment? And then when we grow balls as adolescents the feminists go after those as well and try to take them from us too and castrate us further and emasculate us and turn us into feminized men. And why do you think it is that with all of the awareness about the progressive socio-sexual issues, there is none being created about any of these? That no

136

matter how good women have it, and how bad men have it, the only issues there are any awareness about are women's issues, and men are constantly being censored and silenced when we try to find our voice? Why do you think that there is so much awareness about issues that benefit women and even those which seek to emasculate men, such as transgender issues, but there is nothing being done to protect or promote masculinity. In fact as a man if you speak up and try to protect and promote your own masculinity you are labelled patriarchal, told that you are being "wrong" in some sort of way, stifled, censored, and de-platformed. Women literally try to take us men's voices away using their fascist political power.

Unfortunately for feminism and the misandristic gynocentric world, I have a voice, and I am using it. And all I have left to say at this point is that it just isn't right. It's wrong. It's just wrong. It's pure misandry. And it has to stop. I have never done anything to deserve the type of treatment I have gotten from women. I've always tried to be a good man and do right by them, and what I have gotten in return has been unconscionable. And Men in general do not deserve this type of treatment. Men have never treated women anywhere near as poorly as women treat men, and even when men were generally sexist towards women (which was minute in comparison to the way women treat men these days), that was generations ago and the men of today should not be made to answer for it. Men of today do nothing to oppress women, in fact men at large mostly contribute to women's lives. Most of the value and sustenance and provisions and resources women get from society is coming from men. Men are your farmers, your construction workers and skilled laborers, your business owners, your scientists, your police and military, your legislators and your leaders. Men are the ones who repair your car when it is broken down on the side of the road and you are stranded in the middle of nowhere. Men are the ones saving you and your children's lives when your house is on fire. Men are the ones giving their lives to fight for your freedom and keep you safe so that you can live the luxurious lives in democracy that you do. Men are the ones providing for you to make sure all of your wants and needs are met. Men are the ones giving you children and fathering them (as much as you will let us, or in most cases having our children used against us for extortion). Women don't do these things for men, men do them for women. Imagine if all the men in society went on strike and women had to do these things for themselves, where would you be? You would have nothing without us men to give it to you. And for all the good that we do for you women, all of the self sacrificing, we do not deserve what you do to us in return.

It's bad enough to get taken for granted and used when you have given someone everything that you had to give and gotten nothing in return. But this treatment is so far beyond that. It is senseless abuse. And it is inexcusable and unacceptable. I for one will not stand for it anymore. I am speaking out against all of the female abuse and sexism and I don't care what feminazi's use what kind of shame tactics to try to silence me. I have been silenced with female shame and emotional warfare for years and I won't be silenced anymore. And if you have a problem with me finding my voice and standing up for my rights, let me tell you something, you've got another thing coming. Because I do not have to bend over for you. I'm not the victim you want me to be. Men are not at fault for the things that women blame them for in general, and do not deserve to be villainized just for our gender. It was said that the devil's greatest trick was convincing the world he didn't exist. Well women's greatest trick was convincing the world that misandry doesn't exist, that female on male abuse doesn't exist, and that men are oppressors and women are victims, when in reality it is the opposite. We do not live in a patriarchy, we live in a matriarchy. Men are oppressed by women, not the other way around. And it is time for a paradigm change. It is time for us men to stand up against female abuse and oppression together. Because all of you women's mistreatment isn't doing anything except pushing us over the edge. And now that its gone this far we're starting to fight back. We have men's rights movements starting all over. And you've gone too far now. You've done too much that can't be justified anymore. You've shown your true colors. Shame on you, not us.

Now that feminists and women in general have pushed us far enough, were going to be pushing back. And we are stronger and smarter than you realize. We aren't going to be victimized by you. And we won't be oppressed anymore. In fact the only way you women ever started to win the battle of the sexes was by enlisting men on your side. And now you are going to lose it because you are losing the support of the good men out there who believed in your equality but who you then turned on and tried to dominate and exploit for your own nefarious purposes. You treat us like dogs. Who you try to put into cages and beat into submission. And a dog will only take it so long before it starts to bite back and you find that you've unleashed a beast that you can't control. And who do you think will win in a real competition between men and women? Women always will lose and men always will win. That is the reason why women do not compete against men in sports, and male to female transgendered people are now dominating female sports. You do not want to fight us, there is no competition.

I hope that all of you men out there reading this are with me, and will join me in taking this stand against female tyranny. And I hope that all of you women out there reading this will take this as a warning. Don't fuck with us. You've failed in your goal. Your attempt at a matriarchy has failed. The world is still run by men. Your seductive mind games, manipulations and exploitation is not enough for you to take over control of this world. It is still a patriarchy, not because men are misogynistic, but because men are the ones with the strength and intelligence to build and maintain society. Not women. Women's influence has been nothing but destructive, and you leave it to men to try to rebuild things in your wake. And we can and will stop you if you continue to go too far. Women's influence in society is to bring chaos and destruction. Men's influence is to bring creativity and organization. Patriarchal societies are ones that grow and thrive. When societies become gynocentric they fall, like Rome and Athens. Because women are not forces of organization and control, men are, women are the opposite. And women will destroy society if we let them, as we can see that they already are. But if we men all start rejecting the misandry and double standards of women, they will not be able to continue with them. And if we all start to disengage and go on strike against the gynocentric nature of our culture, it will no longer be able to sustain itself. Women can see their negative effects on society and yet they do not care because it is their nature. And so men have already started to rebel, and the consequences for women are starting to get serious

Remember, we men are the majority of your politicians, your police and military, you're business owners and bosses. We are powerful, and we are in control. And what's more is that you need us more than we need you. Without us men the world would stop. Without us men you women out there would be cat-fighting each other for scraps. All female run businesses and governments fail because not only are they imbalanced but women are not capable of cooperating together or being accountable, objective, or doing other things that it takes to maintain a large stable organization, such as putting in overtime. Women's role in nature and society is to be submissive to and cared for by men. When you try to go against this role you become nothing but lose cannons blowing holes in the infrastructure that men built, without doing anything to help rebuild what you have destroyed. Now it is time for you to stop. Stop your mistreatment of men. Stop your sexism. Stop your war against men. Stop your toxic destructive tendencies. It isn't just, it isn't right, it isn't fair. Men have never treated you the way that you treat us today. And it is time for you to stop. For if you cannot do it of your own accord because it is the right thing to do, we will fight back. And you do not want that. You do not want to see consequences for your actions. But there will be if you continue going down this path.

Already we are seeing men starting to push back. We are seeing that male employers do not want to hire women as much anymore. We are seeing more publicity for female criminals, which means more legislation against them and greater punishments. Men are starting to hit back when a woman strikes them, and other male bystanders are refusing to come to the aid of women who they see attacking men. Men are refusing to pay for women anymore or be used by them, when women have more provisions made for them by society and don't even appreciate what we do for them and only take us for granted. And most of all we are seeing men begin to refuse to marry women, have kids with them, cohabitate with them, or even date them, in astonishing numbers. Men Going Their Own Way is now a mainstream movement. Men are refusing to buy into the hypocritical double standards of women and put up with their misandry anymore. The rebellion against the misandry paradigm has already begun. We men need to continue to cast our votes in favor of ourselves and our best interests and not our oppressors.

Things are no longer going to go women's way if they keep up their hypocrisy and sexism. Rather the opposite. Things will continue to get worse and worse for them. So you'd better learn how to treat us with some god damn mother fucking respect. Because we deserve it.

Because the future is not female like women say, the future is male, just like the past. The society has always been and always will be patriarchal because that is the only way it can sustain itself. After all, you live in a society that men built, which you contribute nothing to, but only take from. You need us and everything that we do for you. Women are not leaders, builders or providers for others, men are. This world you are living in is our house that we have built everything in. You are eating our food, and you do not even cook or clean anymore to help out. And you shouldn't shit where you live, especially if you are not even going to help clean it up. Otherwise you will be ejected like an unwanted guest. And that is what you are in this society. You are all just our guests. And you had better start showing us some appreciation for everything we do for you. Or we will have no incentive to do it anymore.

Women's natural role is one of submission. They were designed by nature for it. They are small and physically far weaker than men, and the hormone estrogen is one that induces passivity and lethargy making their role a more submissive one. It also induces emotional instability and physical health problems, which causes them to require the care of a man, as does pregnancy and child bearing, which is what their body is for. They were not made as strong as men and are not cut out for the types of work that men do. And this paired with their lack of mental stability and organization they are not meant for dominant roles either. The functions that suit them best are ones in which they are serving men and doing more menial tasks. Men are naturally suited for Dominant roles due to the fact that they were designed by nature for them. Their large strong build and the hormone testosterone make them perfect for roles that require aggressiveness, power, leadership, and other forms of Dominance. For both genders to succeed and thrive in society, and for society itself to succeed and thrive as well, we need to keep to the roles that nature intended for us. This is the way that it was traditionally in society before the advent of feminism, and feminism trying to get women to be strong and independent of men and assume more dominant and masculine roles in the world has not helped women to flourish, or be happier, nor has it helped society at large to do so either. Women must regain their place in society as being submissive to men. And if they do so they would find themselves much happier than they have been since feminism has tried to force them to be strong and independent, as studies have shown that women are not as happy as before when they were in their traditionally submissive roles. Because it is unnatural for a woman to not be submissive to men. Women require male Dominance and control and without it they are lost in their own chaos.

Masculinity and its inherent dominance are not toxic as feminists have been saying. In fact it is feminism that is what is toxic, and that is feminism and not femininity. Feminism has poisoned femininity. Masculinity is positive and good. Masculinity is Independent, internally validated and self approved. Masculinity is strong and willful and assertive. Masculinity is rational and logical and reasonable. Masculinity is responsible, accountable and dependable. Masculinity is Dominant, Authoritative and Leading. Masculinity is resourceful and industrious. Masculinity is pro-active and action-taking. Masculinity is driven, ambitious and hard working. Masculinity is ethical, honorable and high integrity. Masculinity is careful conservative and cautious. Masculinity is caregiving, protective, helpful and heroic. Masculinity is confident, courageous and brave. Masculinity is aggressive, violent, dangerous and defensive or offensive when necessary. Masculinity is sexual & creates new life inside of women. Masculinity is free to be whatever the man chooses, and no woman can tell him he is not a real man because he is not doing what she wants, for women do not define masculinity, a man defines his own masculinity. Masculinity is important and essential to society and should not be emasculated. It is socially pro-active and takes initiative with women so that dating and mating can happen. Without it there would be little to no sex acts. There would be little to no children being made. Because we all know that women are not willing or able to make sex happen with men most of the time. Women should appreciate male sexuality and the fact that it has made all of this life in the world happen. For it would not matter that women are the ones who bear the children if their eggs were never getting fertilized by mens sperm, which is exactly what would happen if men weren't Dominant, pro-active and action taking with women. Because women generally do not do so with men (or even start conversations with them or put much effort into them) without our sexual Dominance there would be little to no life on planet earth. So do not take male sexuality for granted, appreciate it. For it is why you exist at all.

Women have responded to these messages when I have posted them on social media, and not with debate, but abuse and ad hominem attacks, such as sexually harassing me and calling me things like "incel". That is the way feminism is, it is not about civil discourse it is about man-hating and oppressing men, and this is why we need to create awareness about this, and why I need your support. And if you are a man who has felt oppressed by these issues I would urge you to please find your voice and join me in taking a stand and speaking out against them. For I cannot do it alone. And so all of that being said, this I'd like to finally conclude this book by leaving you with a poem I wrote about men & their emotions in this anti-male society.

Men Have Feelings

If a man expresses anger he is labelled toxic or a bully

If a man expresses sadness he is labelled weak

If a man cries he is called a pussy or bitch

If a man expresses loneliness, he is labelled a loser or incel

If a man expresses interest he is labelled thirsty or needy

If a man expresses his sexuality he is labelled a player, perv
or creep

If a man expresses love and romantic/emotional commitment
in any way he is labelled clingy

If a man shows any other negative emotions he is told he has
mental issues

If a man is over zealous or expresses a more complex
emotion he is labelled crazy

If a man shows no emotion at all he is called numb, macho, cold, icy, sociopathic, etc

There is literally no way for a man to be emotional without having society at large turning him into a scapegoat and labeling him something horrible. Maybe us men are not the real problem. Maybe it's you, the people who socially condition us to be this way just so you can turn us into your pariah.

We have emotions, we should be allowed to feel them and express them just like you. If you have a problem with that, you can go fuck yourself.

About The Author

Brian Krall is a Social Scientist, former Sex Educator,
an Anti-Feminist, Men's Rights Activist, MGTOW man,
& an author of a dozen books. He is currently single,
living in monk mode in upstate New York.